BOLD
BRILLIANT
— AND —
BAD

Reviews of *WILD IRISH WOMEN*

'A rollicking read'
Books Ireland

'After reading this book, one can never again ignore
the role of Irishwomen'
Dublin Historical Record

'Broderick's prose is simple and accessible, and her fascination
with her two favourite subjects – Irish history and women's studies –
jumps out from every page'
Sunday Business Post

Marian Broderick is a writer and editor who lives and works in London. She is second-generation Irish; her parents are from Donegal and Limerick. She spent every summer of her childhood in Ireland and has developed strong links with the place and the people.
Wild Irish Women: Extraordinary Lives from History proved hugely popular on publication in 2001 and Marian furthered her research to bring the reader more wild Irish women in this volume.

BOLD
BRILLIANT
— AND —
BAD

IRISH WOMEN FROM HISTORY

MARIAN BRODERICK

THE O'BRIEN PRESS
DUBLIN

First published 2018 by

The O'Brien Press Ltd,

12 Terenure Road East, Rathgar, D06 HD27, Dublin 6, Ireland.

Tel: +353 1 4923333; Fax: +353 1 4922777

E-mail: books@obrien.ie

Website: www.obrien.ie

The O'Brien Press is a member of Publishing Ireland.

ISBN: 978-1-78849-018-4

1 3 5 7 9 10 8 6 4 2

18 20 22 23 21 19

Printed and bound by Scandbook AB, Sweden.

The paper in this book is produced using pulp from managed forests.

Published in:

DUBLIN

UNESCO
City of Literature

Dedication

To women across the world, who make their voices heard,
and especially Mary Clement Harkin Broderick, the boldest of them all.

Acknowledgements

Thanks to all my lovely family and friends, particularly Alfredo Cristiano and Conall Broderick Cristiano, Anne Conaghan, Helen Broderick, Tim Collins, Aidan Byrne, Clare Byrne, staff at the London Irish Centre Library in Camden, Colm O'Rourke, Tony Murray, Joanne O'Brien, Sinéad McCoole, Seán Ua Súilleabháin, Tony Kearns, Treasa Harkin of ITMA, staff at the British Library, staff at the National Museum of Ireland, staff at the Royal College of Surgeons in Ireland, Francis Clarke of the National Library of Ireland, John Dunne and all the volunteers at the London Irish Centre Library in Camden Town, Katie Giles of Kingston University Archives, Jacquelyn Borgeson Zimmer and Conrad Froehlich of the Martin and Osa Johnson Safari Museum, Sarah Frandsen of the AELTC, Stephen Weir of the National Museums of Northern Ireland, Rob Gallagher of Sportsfile, Robert O'Connor and Anne O'Neill of An Post, Yvonne Davis and Brendan McGowen of Galway City Museum, Peter Beirne of Clare County Library, Irene Stevenson of *The Irish Times*, Audrey Drohan of UCD, Claire Ní Dhubhcháin of Cnuasach Bhéaloideas Éireann/National Folklore Collection, Legends of America, Jason Flahardy of the University of Kentucky Archives, Sam Cunnington of the Banner of Truth Trust.

Finally thanks to Michael and Ivan O'Brien and all at The O'Brien Press, particularly my hard-working editor Susan Houlden and designer Emma Byrne.

 # CONTENTS

DID YOU KNOWS

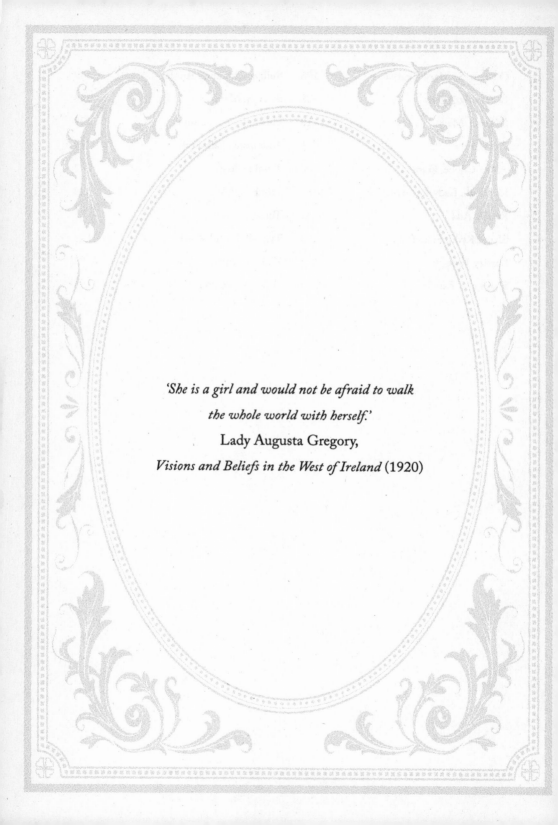

'She is a girl and would not be afraid to walk
the whole world with herself.'
Lady Augusta Gregory,
Visions and Beliefs in the West of Ireland (1920)

INTRODUCTION

Nearly twenty years ago when I wrote *Wild Irish Women*, I walked into a major Irish bookshop and found that no Irish women from the past were represented on its shelves – with the honourable exception of Constance Markievicz.

Fast forward to 2016's Easter Rising commemorations, and I found stories and image of Markievicz and her comrades everywhere, including on buses going down O'Connell Street. Fast forward again to the commemoration of female suffrage in 2018, and there were myriad websites, books, history journals and art projects devoted to giving voice to many women whom history had rendered silent. This is a truly pleasing development – long may it continue into every nook of under-researched Irish history.

In this collection, I aim to continue what I started all those years ago. There are fascinating stories out there about Irish women who are not nationally, let alone internationally, known. Yet they should be household names, tripping off the tongue of every schoolchild and pub-quizzer. First woman in the world to build and fly her own aircraft? Lilian Bland of Co Antrim. Ireland's very own Wild West heroine? Nellie Cashman of Co Cork. Ireland's first international singing star? Catherine Hayes of

Limerick ... the list goes on.

The stories in this book cover subjects from mountaineering to murder, and poetry to philanthropy. These are women in all their multiplicity of layers: political rebels who are also schoolteachers, top sportspeople who are also devoted carers, frontier-busting scientists who are also gifted musicians.

My stories about them are short and snappy; they are intended as an introduction, a tantalizing signpost on the road to finding out more about these women and the times in which they lived. At the end of each section, there is a page of Did You Knows – how many of these women had you heard about?

I have included women from every county in Ireland – and beyond. Emigration has been a cultural phenomenon all too familiar to the Irish, and it features a lot in these pages. Some of my women were second-generation Irish, born of Irish parents in slum conditions abroad. Some were born in Ireland, surrounded by luxury, and could choose whether to stay or go. Many faced the starker choice of leaving or starving, which, as we know, is no choice at all. But nearly all of them travelled and made their mark wherever they went, be it Europe, Asia, Africa or America.

Some of our women were brilliant and some were bad – but they were all bold in their way. I hope the stories avoid the neatly packaged forms of womanhood 'allowed' by society, and show the real women of Ireland's history doing what they did best – living their own lives.

WORLD FIRSTS ...

'I proved wrong the many people who had said
that no woman could build an aeroplane.'
Lilian Bland

Lizzie on the summit of a Norwegian mountain, c.1900.

LIZZIE LE BLOND
1860–1934

Pioneer of mountaineering photography and film

*'For several years it did not occur to me that I could do without a
maid ... I owe a supreme debt of gratitude to the mountains for
knocking from me the shackles of conventionality.'*
Lizzie Le Blond, *Day In, Day Out* (1928)

Elizabeth Hawkins-Whitshed, or Lizzie as she was known, was
born in Dublin, the only child in a titled, military family. She inherited
her father's estate, Killincarrick House in Greystones, on his death, when
she was just eleven years old, but it was held in trust for her until she came
of age at twenty-one. She seemed destined for a life of horse and hounds,
leisure and laziness – but this was not at all what Lizzie had in mind.

Like all rich Victorians girls, Lizzie did not go to school but was educated at home by a governess and claimed it was 'to my ever present regret I
learned absolutely nothing'. She had a London season, as was usual for one
of her social class, and was engaged by the end of it, as was the purpose. The
wedding gifts included those from 'my Irish tenantry' as well as one from
the Prince of Wales.

With her trustees' consent but not approval, at the age of eighteen, Lizzie
married the first of her three husbands, Colonel Fred Burnaby, dubbed 'the

bravest man in England'. Colonel Fred was an adventurer, a practical joker, a daredevil – and doubtless rather hard to live with. After the birth of her son, Harry, Lizzie was advised by doctors to travel abroad to a better climate for her health. 'Travel abroad' was often nineteenth-century code in smart circles for marital separation, and Lizzie and Colonel Fred did not live together again, though she remained on fond terms with her only child's father, and devoted a whole chapter of her autobiography to his many exploits as a soldier.

In Switzerland in 1881, Lizzie became obsessed with mountains. One afternoon she went out with a lady friend, both of them wearing high-heeled boots, and the two somehow managed to make it halfway up Mont Blanc. The experience left Lizzie dazzled. The next time she attempted Mont Blanc, she achieved the summit, and her life course was set.

Taking up climbing, even while wearing a modest, good-quality skirt, horrified relatives in high society. In her autobiography *Day In, Day Out*, Lizzie remembers how 'grand-aunt Lady Bentinck sent out a frantic SOS: "Stop her climbing mountains! She is scandalizing all of London!"'

While she was exploring the Swiss Alps, Lizzie developed another self-taught passion: photography.

It was trying work setting up a camera with half-frozen hands, hiding one's head under a focusing cloth which kept blowing away, and adjusting innumerable screws in a temperature well below freezing-point.

But one learnt one's job very thoroughly.

Lizzie published her pictures in five mountaineering books between

1883 and 1900. Thus she became the world's first mountain photographer. From here, it was a short step to 'animated photography', that is, short films. Her favourite subjects included snow sports, such as tobogganing and skating.

Lizzie published her first book, *The High Alps in Winter*, in 1883 and was self-deprecating about 'the crudest publication of a travel nature ever offered to a kindly public'. However, they were well received by critics.

A different sort of 'book-making' came in 1907 when she discovered eighteenth-century letters between her titled family and European royalty in an old bureau and decided to edit and publish them. She visited German relatives for research, took her own photos of their paintings and jewellery, and edited the manuscript in the same room in which Kaiser Wilhelm was to sign his abdication.

Colonel Fred was killed in action in Sudan in 1885. Lizzie, a fairly merry widow, did not return to any of her homes in London or Ireland but stayed in St Moritz, lavishly funded by the tenantry of her estate in Wicklow.

She took up other sports, such as skating and cycling. Overhearing a man criticising her skating ability one day, she wrote, 'I suppose I have more than my fair share of cussedness, because as soon as that happened I applied myself and became the first woman to pass the highest St Moritz Skating Test.'

She must have had the most astonishing stamina, because she also pushed herself to the limit on cycling, describing how she 'rode from St Moritz most of the way to Rome with my luggage on my machine, carrying my bicycle up over portions of the path along the Lake of Como ...' The advent of the motor car put a stop to this hobby, for obvious safety reasons, which she lamented.

Lizzie made a second, unfortunate marriage in 1886; this time, it was the husband, John Frederick Main, who, after only a year of marriage, went travelling and never came back. Cushioned by her wealth, it seemed to make little difference to her life; she supported him until his death, which, conveniently for her, occurred in 1892.

Her third marriage to Francis Aubrey Le Blond in 1900, when she was forty and he was thirty-one, was the one that lasted the rest of her life. Her husband admired her boundless energy. In 1907 she became foundation president of the Ladies' Alpine Club formed to promote women's climbing. Lizzie and Francis became attracted to Norway because of the previously unconquered mountains and eventually moved there. The two were inveterate travellers, ranging widely from Scandanavia to East Asia and everywhere in between. In 1912 they made a tour of China and Japan returning by the Trans-Siberian Railway. In 1913 it was St Petersburg and Moscow where she experienced a cash-flow problem for possibly the first time in her life: 'The Moscow Bank excelled all others I ever entered in its incompetence,' she wrote acidly.

Despite being Irish, Lizzie saw herself as a woman of the British Empire, as did many of her class. During World War I, she went to France to work as a hospital volunteer in Dieppe, and she raised funds for ambulances. Just after the war she travelled with her camera around what she called the 'tortured trenches' and raised money to restore the damaged medieval Reims Cathedral.

Lizzie's final decade was spent involved in the post-war relationship between France and Britain, and writing her witty, name-dropping autobiography, *Day In, Day Out*, complete with frontispiece of her looking resplendent in tiara and feathers, and with a foreword by EF Benson of *Mapp and Lucia* fame.

Shortly before she died, Lizzie was awarded the Légion d'honneur in France for her efforts in getting a statue of the Allied Commander-in-Chief, Marshall Foch, erected in London's Belgravia, where it still stands. She died in Wales after an operation, aged seventy-two, and is buried in Brompton Cemetery, London.

Lizzie, wearing full skirts, climbing in the Swiss Alps.

LILIAN BLAND
1878–1971

First woman in the world to design, build and fly an aircraft

*'I had proved wrong the many people who had said that no
woman could build an aeroplane, and that
gave me great satisfaction …'*
Lilian Bland, *Western Morning News* (1966)

Initiative, guts and determination, Lilian had all the qualities to make a great design engineer in the early 1900s. All, that is, except one: she wasn't born a man.

Lilian was born in Kent but came from a long line of Anglo-Irish gentry, and, when her mother died, her family moved back to their roots in Carnmoney, Co Antrim. Lilian experienced this move as liberating and she made the most of it, indulging her love of hunting, shooting, and fishing.

She was attracted to the world of photography, and became an excellent photographer, doing all her own chemical processing and fixing. She also avidly followed one of the biggest stories in the papers at the time: the progress of the Wright brothers of America and of Louis Blériot of France, who had finally managed powered, controlled flight, and patented their own aircrafts. Lilian devoured the stories and, by 1908, she had become obsessed with flying.

Lilian at the controls of **Mayfly**, *which she designed, built and flew in 1910.*

Having read everything she could lay her hands on, Lilian travelled to England to a meeting of amateur aviators. She made detailed observations of all that she saw, from the techniques of the aviators to the dimensions of their aircraft. Back in Antrim, she asked her aunt for access to her uncle's workshop. And it was here that Lilian started to design her own flying machine.

She used local and imported timber, and recycled materials where she could. After several successful smaller models, which she flew as large kites, Lilian embarked on a full-size glider with a wingspan of over 6 m (20 ft). It was an ambitious project and Lilian had a gallows sense of humour: she named her creation *Mayfly* – after an insect that lives for one day only.

In early 1910, the day dawned when Lilian was ready to take *Mayfly* to the top of Carnmoney Hill. The idea was that thermal currents would lift the aircraft from the top of the hill and it would glide down the hillside for some distance. Wisely Lilian persuaded five men to hang off *Mayfly* as ballast rather than doing it herself. *Mayfly's* maiden flight worked like a dream, and the men landed safely, which led Lilian to conclude that if *Mayfly* could bear the weight of five men, it could bear the weight of an engine.

She brought a two-stroke engine over from England and fitted it in the workshop. By the summer of 1910, after a few adjustments, the new engine-powered *Mayfly* was ready. This time Lilian wanted to fly it herself.

She moved this final phase of her operation to the Randalstown estate of Baron O'Neill in Co Antrim, because it had a huge field, albeit shared with his lordship's bull. Lilian mounted and strapped herself in; an assistant was standing by. The plane's engine roared and kangaroo-hopped across the field, stopping the hearts of Lilian's father and other spectators.

But the *Mayfly* did become airborne to about thirty feet (nine metres). Lilian had become the first woman in the world to design, build and fly her own aircraft.

From a commercial perspective, Lilian's planes and gliders were not a success. She knew she needed a bigger engine, but she also knew a bigger engine would wreck the plane. Surprisingly she seems to have taken no further interest in aircraft, but she was able to maintain her interest in engines by turning to the new world of motor vehicles. In due course she worked as an agent for the motor car, the Model T by Henry Ford.

The year after her flying triumph, Lilian married her cousin Charles Loftus Bland and embarked on a completely different life. The couple settled in Quatsino, a remote area of British Columbia, Canada. Lilian gave birth to her only child, Patricia, and the family worked hard to build a life. They had little success, struggling continually with failed ventures and money troubles. Then, when Patricia was only sixteen, she died of a tetanus infection. Lilian's marriage collapsed after the tragedy and she left Canada for good. She spent the rest of her long life in England, keeping busy with her gardening and horse-racing, and she died aged ninety-two, in Cornwall.

Today there is a park named after Lilian Bland in Glengormley, Newtownabbey, Co Antrim, featuring a full-size sculpture of her plane.

KAY McNULTY
1921–2006

Co-inventor of the first general-use digital computer

'Science and everyday life cannot and should not be separated.'
Rosalind Franklin, *c.*1940

From a Donegal fishing village to the heart of American wartime intelligence, the trajectory of Kay McNulty's life journey was an unusual one.

Kathleen, known as Kay, was born in the townland of Feymore, near Creeslough, in the Donegal Gaeltacht, an Irish-speaking part of north-west Ireland. She was the daughter of stone mason and IRA officer, James McNulty. He was arrested and imprisoned for two years when Kay was just a baby. When he was released in 1924, he and his wife Anne and their six children emigrated to Pennsylvania. Kay had to learn English in America before going to school.

Kay was always a maths whizz, graduating at the top of every class through-out school. When the USA got involved in the war in 1941, Kay was still attending Chestnut Hill College for Women. She graduated with a degree in mathematics in 1942 and went straight into helping with the war effort.

She accepted a role at the University of Pennsylvania in Philadelphia, where her job was to improve the range and accuracy of American artil-lery by making mathematical calculations about current trajectories. Kay

Kay McNulty, c.1942.

and her female colleagues worked on hand-operated calculators and they themselves were known as 'computers'.

Wartime speeds up technology, and soon Kay was shown an enormous, brand-new, top-secret invention named ENIAC (Electronic Numerical Integrator and Computer), which had been co-created by her future husband and physicist John Mauchly. This was the world's first electronic digital computer and, along with five other women, Kay got the job of writing the programme for it. This was before the advent of any such thing as computer science, so essentially Kay and her colleagues taught themselves how to do programming. Her programme slashed the human time of making the trajectory calculations from thirty or forty hours to up to four calculations per minute.

Kay married John Mauchly in 1948 and became stepmother to his two

Kay McNulty (left) and colleagues operating an early computer, University of Pennsylvania, c.1942–1945.

children, as well as going on to have five children of her own. She continued to work as a software designer for her husband's inventions. In later life she also wrote and lectured on software engineering. Unfortunately Kay was widowed in her late fifties; she remarried but was widowed a second time in her seventies.

Her achievements in computer science as a young woman having been forgotten, Kay started to receive recognition in later life. In 1986 the Letterkenny Institute of Technology in her home county of Donegal introduced a medal, the Kay McNulty Mauchly Antonelli medal, to be presented annually to a computer science student. She visited the college in 1999. In 1997 she and the other five women who programmed ENIAC were inducted into the Women in Technology International Hall of Fame. In 2017 Dublin City University named a computing facility after her.

Kay died in 2006 in Pennsylvania. She was eighty-five.

DID YOU KNOW?

* * *

The academic **Agnes O'Farrelly** (1874–1951) from Virginia, Co Cavan, was the first woman to write a series of novels in Irish. She did not speak Irish until she was an adult but, despite this late start, she went on to replace Douglas Hyde as Professor of Modern Irish at University College Dublin (UCD).

* * *

Co Galway woman **Alice Perry** (1885–1969) was the first female in Europe to graduate with an engineering degree. She worked as a county surveyor in Ireland, then a factory inspector in England. After losing her husband of six months in World War I, she became a Christian Scientist and moved to the USA.

* * *

In 1955, Belfast-born crooner **Ruby Murray** (1935–1996) was the first person to have five songs simultaneously in the Top Twenty. This record stood for more than fifty years before it was equalled in 2009 by Michael Jackson.

* * *

In 1921 **Mary O'Toole** (1874–1954) of Carlow became one of the world's first female judges when she was appointed to the law court in Washington DC, USA. With tongue-in-cheek, she was quoted in *The Washington Times* of 27 January 1921, saying that women jurors needed breaks to powder their noses because they couldn't 'think straight with shiny faces'.

* * *

... AND IRISH FIRSTS

'Being a woman is like being Irish;
everyone says you're important and nice,
but you take second place all the time.'
Iris Murdoch

DR EMILY WINIFRED DICKSON

1866–1944

First woman Fellow of the Royal College of
Surgeons in Ireland (FRCSI)

'An epidemic ... of Lady Medicals has broken out
in a certain hospital in town.'
St Stephen's: A Record of University Life (1903)
reporting on Richmond Hospital, Dublin,
employing three women

Emily Winifred Dickson must have lost count of the times she collided with gender discrimination in an effort simply to do a job she loved and for which she was well suited.

She was born the second-youngest of seven children in Dungannon, Co Tyrone. Emily's father became a Liberal MP when she was eight, by which time her mother was an invalid. Emily went to boarding school in Belfast and London, and took over her mother's nursing care after leaving school. Her application to go to Trinity College was vetoed by the theological faculty, which didn't want to accept women.

In 1887 Emily applied and was accepted to the Royal College of Surgeons

Dr Emily Winifred Dickson on graduation day, 1891.

in Ireland (RCSI), where she was the only woman student on the roll. By 1891 she had obtained her first-class certificate from here and her licence from the Royal College of Physicians of Ireland (RCPI). She trained in midwifery at Dublin's Rotunda Hospital. In the 1890s, it wasn't easy; medicine was a job for the well off because medical students had to gain clinical experience at their own cost – for example, paying Dublin hospitals, such as Sir Patrick Dun's, to take them on ward visits.

In 1893 Emily graduated from the Royal University of Ireland and in the same year she was elected a Fellow of the Royal College of Surgeons in Ireland (FRCSI). She was the first woman in Ireland or Britain to achieve this; it was not until 1920 that London appointed a female FRCS.

Emily decided to continue specialising in midwifery and gynaecology – not, one might think a particularly controversial choice for a woman. But when she was awarded a six-month travelling scholarship to continue training in Berlin, she came up against male disapproval and was barred from doing ward rounds with other doctors because she was a woman.

After completing her scholarship, Emily returned to Dublin and set up her practice at 18 Upper Merrion St. Again, she collided with authority when she was refused a licence to practise at the Rotunda on the basis of her gender. However she managed to find employment in other hospitals, including the Coombe.

Through these years Emily not only lectured and published papers on gynaecology, but organised a committee to help women students with accommodation in Dublin. She completed two post-graduate degrees in medicine and obstetrics, becoming a Doctor of Medicine and Master of Obstetrics at the Royal University of Ireland in 1896. Despite this, when she was made an examiner, there was a petition by outraged male students intent on preventing a woman from examining them. The petition failed.

'Woman,' she wrote, 'should not give up the medical profession for the profession of marriage unless she likes the latter profession better.' Yet Emily did just that. When, aged thirty-three, she married Robert McGregor Martin, she gave up medicine for fifteen years. Emily's marriage produced five children.

After World War I broke out and Emily's husband joined up, Emily regarded a return to medicine as her patriotic duty, and unusually, used her maiden name professionally.

With all the children except the youngest at boarding schools, she moved to England. She worked mainly in Lancashire in much less senior roles than she'd had in Ireland.

After the war, life became more difficult for Emily. Her husband returned with severe shellshock. This led Emily to become involved in psychiatry, an area that interested her for the rest of her life. Emily nursed her husband but herself fell victim to the Spanish Influenza epidemic, which swept the world in 1918–19, and is estimated to have killed 25 million people – more people than died during four years of war. Her health never fully recovered. She developed the painful and crippling disease of rheumatoid arthritis, and her ability to work was affected.

Emily spent the inter-war period travelling and working when she could. She returned to Lancashire during World War II, and was still active in psychiatry when she died of cancer, aged seventy-seven years old.

In 2012, papers belonging to Dr Dickson were donated to RCSI by her grandson, Dr Niall Martin. These papers included certificates, testimonials, medals, correspondence and photographs dating from the 1880s–1920s. The papers are now catalogued in the RCSI Library.

In 2016 the RCSI created an award in Emily's honour. Today the Emily Winifred Dickson award is given to women who have made an outstanding contribution in their field.

BEATRICE HILL-LOWE

1868–1951

First Irishwoman to win an Olympic medal

*'The most important thing in the Olympic Games is not winning
but taking part; the essential thing in life is not conquering
but fighting well.'*

Pierre de Coubertin, founder of the modern Olympics

It was a sweltering July day in the White City Stadium, London, and the 1908 Olympic medal ceremony for Women's Archery was underway. Gold went to Britain, silver went to Britain, and bronze went to Britain – but the recipient of the bronze medal was, in fact, an Irishwoman, forty-year-old Beatrice Hill-Lowe from Ardee, Co Louth, and this historic moment marked the first but not the last time an Irishwoman was to win an Olympic medal.

Beatrice Ruxton was born one of eight children in a substantial mansion named Ardee House on New Year's Day 1868. Her family had been Anglo-Irish Ascendency since the 1600s and her father was a representative of the Crown in the county. Beatrice grew up in a world firmly entrenched in all the privilege of centuries. She was married in 1891, at the age of twenty-three,

Beatrice Hill–Lowe.

to a Commander Hill-Lowe of the Royal Navy, another pillar of the establishment, and considerably older than his wife. They had no children.

Archery was one of the very few sports considered suitable for a woman: it didn't involve running or other tomboyish movement, it was graceful, and it was played while fully clothed. It was also a well-to-do sport, requiring as it did expensive equipment and a piece of private land to practise on. It is not known how Beatrice took it up but, as a rich young woman, she certainly would already have been able to ride, and probably played tennis and croquet. In fact these sports, along with golf and sailing, had been open to women since the Paris Olympics in 1900. Archery was opened to women participants only in 1904.

In 1908 there was no Irish Olympic team because the whole island of Ireland was still under British rule, and Irish athletes had to compete under the Union Jack. There were many and varied protests about the continuing failure by the British government to grant Home Rule to Ireland. One such was the boycotting by many Irish athletes of the London Olympics of 1908. They were not the only ones: the American Olympic team (which included a high proportion of Irish Americans) marked the event with their own protest when they refused

Beatrice Hill-Lowe's Olympic bronze.

to tip their flag to Britain's royal box.

But Beatrice was not of this ilk. She held no qualms about competing under the Union Jack and gave a creditable performance at 50 yards and then again at 60 yards, beaten into third place by two legendary English-women, Sybil 'Queenie' Newall (at fifty-three still the oldest woman ever to win an Olympic medal) and the extraordinary all-rounder Charlotte 'Lottie' Dod, who, as well as her Olympic silver for archery, was a member of the national hockey team, a British golf champion, and won five Wimbledon singles titles.

After her Olympic achievement, Beatrice retreated into a quiet life. The Hill-Lowes moved to Shropshire, where Beatrice's elderly husband died. She married again and never went back to live in Ireland. She died in Pembrokeshire, North Wales, in 1951 aged eighty-three.

The silver quiver that Beatrice used in the 1908 Olympics.

DAME IRIS MURDOCH

1919–1999

Novelist, first Irish writer to win the Booker prize

'Being a woman is like being Irish; everyone says you're important and nice, but you take second place all the time.'
Iris Murdoch, *The Red and the Green* (1965)

A prolific novelist and philosopher, Iris was born in 1919 in Dublin, the only child of a middle-class Protestant couple. When she was just a few weeks old the family moved from Phibsborough, north Dublin, to London, where her father had taken a job.

Iris was privately educated and after school attended Somerville College, Oxford. While there, she joined the Communist Party. Although she left the party a few years later, her erstwhile membership dogged her. Whenever she tried to visit America, she had to obtain special permission from the US government, even during the most successful years of her writing career.

After graduating, Iris was conscripted to work in a series of well-heeled administrative roles in the Treasury and the United Nations. In 1948, she started teaching at St Anne's, Oxford, where she became a Fellow. From here, Iris started to write.

Iris Murdoch in later life.

She published a work of philosophy before she published fiction; her debut novel was *Under the Net* (1954). She went on to write twenty-five novels, winning major prizes. She won the James Tait Black Memorial Prize for *The Black Prince* (1973) and the Whitbread Prize for Fiction for *The Sacred and Profane Love Machine* (1974). She won the Booker in 1978 for *The Sea, The Sea*, the first (though not the last) Irish-born writer to do so. As well as at least one novel every two or three years, Iris also published two plays, one anthology of poetry and several books on philosophy through the 1960s and '70s.

In 1956 Iris married an Oxford don, John Bayley. They were a successful intellectual pairing. Iris was bisexual and, with her husband's knowledge, maintained affairs with both sexes throughout her long marriage. The couple had no children.

Latterly Iris rejected much about her Irish heritage. Some of her early works, such as *The Red and the Green* (1965) were set during the War of Independence and treated sympathetically protagonists from both sides of the conflict. However, she later came to regret being seen as endorsing Irish nationalism. Later, she described how unIrish she felt and referred to her heritage in less than flattering terms. She was made a Dame Commander of the Order of the British Empire in 1987.

A biopic named *Iris* (made in 2001) depicts beautifully the cruel descent of a prolific intellectual into Alzheimer's disease from the point of view of her loyal husband and latterly carer, John Bayley. Iris Murdoch died of Alzheimer's in her beloved Oxford in 1999.

DID YOU KNOW?

* * *

The folklorist **Charlotte Brooke** (1740–1793) was born in Rantavan, Co Cavan, one of twenty-two children. She is credited as being the first to collect scattered poems in the Irish language, which she published in the original, alongside translations in English. She also published a Gaelic language magazine *Bolg tSolair* in the 1790s.

* * *

The antiquarian **Lady Harriet Kavanagh** (1799–1885) of Borris House, Co Carlow, was the first Irishwoman to travel around Egypt, which she achieved largely on camel-back.

* * *

The first compilation of famous Irish women in book form was published in 1877. *Illustrious Irishwomen* was written by **Elizabeth Casey**, aka **E Owens Blackburne** (1845–94), from Slane, Co Meath.

* * *

Born in France, **Louise Gavan Duffy** (1884–1969) first encountered the Irish language as a teenager at her father Charles Gavan Duffy's funeral. She studied it until she was fluent, then founded Ireland's first Irish language school, Scoil Bhríde Girls' School in Earlsfort Terrace, Dublin. As a member of Cumann na mBan, she was in the GPO during the Easter Rising.

* * *

Cork city woman **Margaret Buckley** (1885–1962) was the first female leader of any political party in Ireland. She was president of Sinn Féin from 1937 to 1950 and had the distinction of being imprisoned by both the British and the Irish Free State.

Averill Deverell (1893–1979) from Greystones, Co Wicklow, was the first woman in either Ireland or Britain to practise as a barrister. She became known as the 'Mother of the Bar' and her portrait hangs in Dublin's Law Library.

In October 1980, Dublin-born **Mella Carroll** (1934–2006) became the first woman judge to be appointed to the High Court of Ireland.

Four Courts, Dublin.

SPORTING CHAMPIONS

'For Christmas I didn't want a doll,

I wanted a football!'

Anne O'Brien

LENA RICE
1866–1907

The only Irishwoman ever to win a singles title at Wimbledon

*'We have been told of serious constitutional disturbance having
developed itself in young married women from overmuch lawn
tennis, but of this we desire to speak with bated breath.'*

Nineteenth-century periodical

The year 1890 was stellar for Irish tennis, because, in the summer
of that year, no fewer than three Wimbledon lawn tennis titles, plus the US
Open women's, were won by Irish players. Lena Rice was among their number.

Helena 'Lena' Rice was born to a wealthy family at Marlhill, near New
Inn, close to Cashel in Co Tipperary. She had three brothers and four sisters, and from a young age played tennis with her sister Annie, who was
three years older. Tennis was just taking off as a sport – one of the few that
was considered suitable for young women, played, as it was, in full-length
skirts and corsets. Tennis parties in the late-nineteenth century were social
occasions and a good place to develop courtships. Lena and her sister Anne
were encouraged by their parents to become members of the Cahir Lawn
Tennis Club.

Athletic culture was the pastime of the leisured classes and tennis
tournaments were largely run by and for amateurs. Lena and Annie were

Lena Rice, in action on the tennis court, c.1890.

Tipperary's very own Venus and Serena Williams for a while; they won everything locally and then together entered the high-status Irish Championship, run by the Fitzwilliam Lawn Tennis Club in May 1889. (This club had outgrown its original home in Upper Pembroke Street, off Fitzwilliam Square, Dublin, and had moved to Wilton Place. But the Irish Championship tournament was still played in the original venue.) The tournament was the first tennis tournament in the world to admit ladies' singles and mixed doubles titles – and the ladies' matches were played in private to preserve their dignity.

Lena acquitted herself creditably in this her first outing in a major tournament. She was beaten by her English arch-rival Blanche Hillyard in the singles semi-final. She reached the finals alongside Blanche in the women's doubles, but went on to beat her in the mixed doubles to win the title.

At the end of June both Annie and Lena played at the Lansdowne Lawn Tennis Club tournament where they both lost their singles matches to a Miss G Crofton, although Lena managed to make it through to the final. Annie beat her sister in the semi-final of the mixed doubles, but they came away with nothing.

A week later, the sisters both competed at Wimbledon and both faced the reigning champion, Blanche. Blanche disposed of Annie in the opening round and took on Lena in the final. It was a famous fight between the two – Blanche afterwards described it as her most memorable match. Blanche won 6-4, 6-8, 4-6, making Lena the runner-up. As a consolation prize, Lena made history towards the end of the competition by becoming the first woman to officiate as a lineswoman in the men's singles.

The following year, 1890, Lena attended the same three tournaments. She was runner-up in the Irish Championship women's singles event, and put on an excellent show at Lansdowne Road, winning the singles with ease. By the time she crossed the sea to compete at Wimbledon, she was on top form.

'The year of the Irish' at the Wimbledon tournament saw Frank Stoker (cousin to Bram Stoker, the creator of Count Dracula) and Joshua Pim, from Dublin and Wicklow respectively, winning the men's doubles, while Willoughby Hamilton from Kildare won the men's singles.

As for Lena, she had a stroke of luck. Her arch-rival, Blanche, was pregnant and didn't compete, leaving the way clear for Lena. Correctly attired in a long skirt, long-sleeved shirt, boater hat and tie, Lena faced May Jacks on the Centre Court. She won a very convincing 6-4, 6-1 to bring home the Challenge Trophy – and invented a move now known as the forearm smash in the process. With her prize money of 20 guineas Lena bought a stunning diamond and emerald ring.

Unfortunately after this triumph, domestic duty imposed itself on Lena. Her mother was sick, and although Lena had many siblings, she was a single woman and expected to care for her, which she did.

The death of her mother in March 1891 made the defence of her Wimbledon title that summer impossible for Lena. We can only imagine how painful it must have been to know that the tournament was proceeding without her, and that her rival Blanche Hillyard had made it to the final. There is every possibility that the twenty-five-year-old Lena could have retained her title. Blanche was comprehensively beaten by Lottie Dod 6-2, 6-1.

There is no record of Lena ever playing tennis again. The Wimbledon winner's career had lasted just two years. She lived quietly at home for the rest of her short life, and died in 1907 of tuberculosis of the hip on her forty-first birthday.

KAY MILLS

1923–1996

The most decorated player in the history of Gaelic games

'She was an iconic camogie player and an amazing woman.'
Phyllis Breslin, former president of the
Irish Camogie Association

Kathleen Rosaleen Mills was born in Inchicore, Dublin, but her mother died when she was a baby. Her father worked for the Irish railroads known then as the Great Southern Railway (GSR) and now as Iarnród Éireann (IÉ), and Kay was mainly raised by her grandmother. She came young to the women's sport of camogie, discovering a love of the game while still at convent school.

According to *A Game of Our Own: A History of Camogie* (2011) by Mary Moran, camogie emerged in 1903 as part of the Gaelic revival of the 1890s. A woman named Máire Ní Chinnéide, aka Mary Kennedy, based the rules of the new women's game on the men's traditional sport of hurling. (Máire was herself an exceptional person, a talented linguist, a professor of Irish – who played in the first camogie match and was the first woman ever to score a goal in competitive camogie. She was also a playwright for Dublin's Peacock Theatre, and she was the first woman to be President of Oireachtas na Gaeilge – the Irish culture festival.)

The Tailteann Games of 1928 and 1932 heightened the profile of camogie and encouraged players to compete at a national as well as club level. In 1932, the first All-Ireland Championship was held.

By the time Kay was fourteen, in 1937, she was part of the camogie team attached to the Great Southern Railway's Athletic Union, paid for by the workers. Tall and slim, here she honed her left-handed style. Playing in local Dublin matches, she became known for her turn of speed and her competitive resilience, and she was soon promoted.

When she was just seventeen years old, Kay was asked to make her debut for the Dublin Senior Team in the All-Ireland final; Dublin lost against Cork. The following year she played against Cork in the 1942 All-Ireland final and this time Dublin won. (There must have been much wry humour in the Mills household about this, since Kay's father was a Cork man!) This victory garnered Kay her first All-Ireland medal, and national attention for her beautiful style of playing. Her team successfully defended their title over the following two years. Kay's career had taken off.

Kay married in 1947, but kept her maiden name for camogie. The 1950s were her decade. By 1957 she had won no fewer than eleven All-Ireland finals, and in 1958 she was made Dublin's captain. Apparently invincible, she then led Dublin in an unbroken run of four victories from 1958 to 1961. By now, as Moran says, she was seen as Ireland's first camogie superstar.

In 1961, at the age of thirty-eight, and having won the All-Ireland yet again, Kay retired. Her final tally was fifteen All-Ireland Senior medals, twenty Leinster Championships, six Dublin Championships and four inter-provincial medals. It is a record that no hurler or Gaelic footballer, male or female, has yet equalled.

In retirement Kay lived a quiet, unassuming life. She was honoured post-humously when the All-Ireland Junior Camogie Cup was renamed for her. As a famous Dubliner, she was also shortlisted to have a new bridge over the Liffey in Dublin named after her – but was narrowly beaten by trade unionist Rosie Hackett. There is a plaque on her home in Inchicore that describes her playing style: 'Lithe and graceful, a superb midfield player with neat wrist work; quick to lift and strike at full speed, she could score from any angle.'

Kay Mills hoisting the original O'Duffy cup, presented to the winners of the All-Ireland Senior Camogie Championship.

PHILOMENA GARVEY

1926–2009

Golfing champion

'As an Irish woman I feel it would have been disloyal to my
country were I to accept and wear such an emblem
[as the Union Jack] alone on my blazer.'

Phil Garvey on her withdrawal from the Curtis Cup (1958)

Born in the village of Baltray, Co Louth, on 26 April 1926, Philomena 'Phil' Garvey led a quiet but determined life – and dominated women's golf for twenty-four years; she is still regarded as the best woman golfer Ireland has ever seen.

Phil was the youngest of a family of six children, and the Garveys lived close to the County Louth Golf Club. Consequently, all the children played to a good standard; Phil started playing when she was six or seven years old.

After attending school in Drogheda, Phil went to work in Dublin. Her longest-standing job was in the sports section in Clery's famous department store (now sadly closed) on Dublin's O'Connell Street. (Later she

Philomena Garvey practising for the Curtis Cup, 1952.

would come to an arrangement with the management that allowed her to take unpaid leave in the summer months to concentrate on her golf.)

At the age of twenty, in 1946, Phil won the Irish Ladies' Amateur Golf Championship. It was the first of an astonishing fifteen wins in all, an unbeaten tally to this day. She was also a finalist for the first time in the British Ladies' Amateur Golf Championship at Hunstanton, England, the same year. She made the finals in this prestigious tournament five times in total. Her finest hour came in 1957 at Gleneagles, in Scotland, when she won the championship.

In 1947 Phil represented her country at the Home Internationals, and continued to do so over a period of twenty-two years, missing just five years, due to ineligibility or injury.

In team tournaments, Phil was part of the winning team twice in the Vagliano Trophy. She was selected for the prestigious tournament, the Curtis Cup (representing Britain and Ireland against the Americans), six times and won it twice, in 1952 and 1956. But in 1958, the year after her Gleneagles victory, Phil told the Curtis Cup organizers that she could not agree to wear a blazer decorated solely with the Union Jack badge, because it was not representative of the Irish and, as she stated later, she was an Irish woman, and from a country with a flag of its own. She suggested, as a compromise, that she wear the older team badge, which featured the shamrock, thistle, leek and rose, representing all four home countries. This sensible suggestion was rejected, and the Ladies' Golf Union (LGU) organisers denied her the opportunity to play. The Irish Ladies' Golf Union (ILGU) objected and their president even offered to resign in support of Phil. When she was selected again the following year, the LGU reconsidered and the badge was changed.

From 1964 to 1967, Phil played as a professional, the first Irishwoman to do so, but was re-admitted into amateur ranks in 1968, and won her last Irish Championship two years later. She retired from playing in 1970 at the top of her game; according to her biographer, Paul Garvey, she embodied the motto of the Garvey coat-of-arms, *Morior Invictus*, or To Die Unconquered.

Despite retirement, she made many more contributions to the world of golf, writing a newspaper column and acting as a selector, although she used a wheelchair for periods due to mobility problems.

In 2007 Phil and her family marked the fiftieth anniversary of her great win at the British Ladies' Amateur Golf Championship. Two years later, on the eve of a long-planned event at her beloved local golf club, Phil died suddenly, aged eighty-three. At her funeral, the current president, past presidents, and members of the ILGU, who had made her a life vice-president, formed a Guard of Honour.

ANNE O'BRIEN
1956–2016

First woman footballer from Ireland or Britain to sign for a professional European women's team

'For Christmas I didn't want a doll, I wanted a football!'
Anne O'Brien

Footballing pioneer, Anne O'Brien was at the vanguard of a movement that now sees more investment and interest than ever before – women's football.

Anne was born in Inchicore, Dublin, part of a large, sporty family. Her father, brothers and first cousins were all involved in playing football, so Anne's first matches were with them, when she was aged about ten.

Her first women's team was made up of the factory girls from a Dublin fur company. They played in Dublin's Phoenix Park and they won almost every match Anne played in. She then played for the Dublin All-Stars. In 1973 the management of a French team, Stade de Reims, arrived in Dublin on a scouting trip. They organised some games with Anne's team, and quickly spotted her talent as a midfielder. After seeking her mother's permission, they took her around Ireland to play in more games, in several of which Anne scored impressively. That was enough. Stade de Reims were the best women's club in the world at the time, and they wanted to sign up

Anne O'Brien (second left) with Stade de Reims manager and teammates.

Anne. She became the first woman from either Ireland or Britain to play professionally in Europe. She had just turned eighteen.

The rest of Anne's career was spent abroad. She took just nine months to become fluent in French and won a league title in her time with Stade de Reims. When after three years, she moved to Rome to play for Lazio, she easily made the transition to speaking Italian. Anne credited the Irish classes she'd had at school for this; being taught Irish at a young age had given her a knack for other languages.

The 1970s and '80s saw the growth of the women's game, with plenty of money and sponsorship available. During a career lasting over twenty years, Anne clocked up five Scudetti (league titles) and two national Women's Coppa Italia trophies. She continued to play while she was in the early stages of pregnancy with her only child, a son named Andrea (who also became a professional footballer). She returned to the game just weeks after his birth, and used to breastfeed him at half-time. She was proud that three of her five league titles were won after she became a mother.

She had represented her own country just four times as a fifteen- and sixteen-year-old but, after she left, she played for Ireland in Dublin just once more in a UEFA Women's Euro qualifier against the Netherlands in 1990. She said somewhat wistfully that the national squad never came looking for her, although she would have been honoured to play. (This omission on the part of the Irish was due mainly to cost constraints in the women's game at the time.) Rome became her permanent home because, she said, 'The Roman people are like Dublin people; they're blackguards and they like living the life!'

Anne hung up her football boots in 1994, aged thirty-eight. In retirement, she worked with Italian under-17s, scouting and arranging games and tournaments. She loved going home to Ireland but always appreciated the chance that life had given her.

'It's not about just playing football,' she said. 'You get to travel, meet people, learn other cultures – it makes life richer.'

She died prematurely in Rome, aged only sixty.

DID YOU KNOW?

* * *

From 1912 to 1948 the modern Olympic Games featured an art competition. **Letitia Hamilton** (1878–1964) from Co Meath won a bronze medal for her painting *Meath Hunt Point-to-Point* in 1948.

* * *

Tennis champ **Mabel Cahill** (1863–1905) emigrated from Kilkenny to New York as a young woman, where she took the tennis world by storm. She won the United States Championships singles event in 1891. In 1892, the only non-American woman playing, she won singles, women's doubles and mixed doubles at the same tournament, making her the first player to win the 'triple crown' at a major tennis tournament.

* * *

Pioneering educator **Sophie Bryant**, neé Willock (1850–1922), of Dublin was not only a head mistress, author, suffragette and Home Rule activist, but also a well-respected mountaineer. She died in an avalanche on Mont Blanc, aged seventy-two.

* * *

THE LIFE
SCIENTIFIC

*'I feel like the Queen of Sheba when she realized the glory
and the wisdom of Solomon …'*
Mary Ward

THE HONOURABLE MARY WARD

1827–1869

Microscopist

'When I think of these things, I feel like the Queen of Sheba when she realized the glory and the wisdom of Solomon ... It is like seeing a faint glimpse of the meaning of "infinite Power".'
Mary Ward, *A World of Wonders Revealed by the Microscope* (1858)

At a time when girls were not meant to be educated in science – or indeed in anything much at all – Mary Ward, née King, became a leading, self-taught microscopist.

Born in Ferbane, Co Offaly, Mary's father Henry King was a clergyman and keen amateur scientist. A maternal cousin, William Parsons, 3rd Earl of Rosse, became famous as the builder of 'The Leviathan', the then-largest telescope in the world in 1845. (Today, a restored version of this can be seen at Birr Castle, which is still occupied by descendants of the same family).

Influenced by her cousin and her father, the young Mary developed a precocious interest in science. She examined insects through a magnifying glass and made exquisite drawings of them. She acquired a microscope and

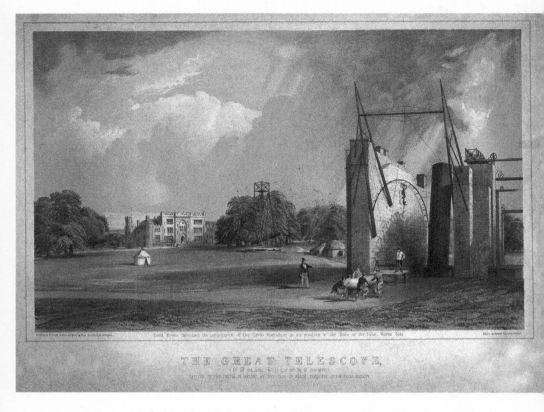

THE GREAT TELESCOPE,

The detailed drawings that Mary made of the famous 'Leviathan' telescope at Birr Castle were used in its reconstruction.

placed herself on a strict schedule of independent study into microscopy.

Cousin William, being a male, had been allowed to study at a university, while Mary had to keep up with him by studying at home. When William became President of the Royal Society in 1849, Mary made use of her connection, meeting many scientists as a result.

In 1854 at the age of twenty-seven, Mary married Henry Ward, Viscount Bangor, and changed from Miss King to the Honourable Mrs Mary Ward. They had eight children. By the time of her marriage, Mary was an acknowledged expert on microscopy, and during the rest of her short life published a number of lively books on the subject. These include *A Windfall for the Microscope* (1856), *Sketches with the Microscope* (1857), *A World of Wonders Revealed by the Microscope* (1858), *Telescope Teachings* (1859), *Microscope Teachings* (1864), and 'The Natterjack Toad in Ireland' (1864).

Some of these works were intended for children – one is addressed to 'Dear Emily' as an extended letter – and they are strikingly clear and accessible, more than 170 years later. Mary illustrated them all herself in colour. These publications were a boost to her independence and reputation, and the scientific community grudgingly accepted she was doing valuable work. Not only was she allowed to become a subscriber to Royal Society resources (one of only three women to do so), but she was also permitted to visit the hallowed Royal Observatory at Greenwich, previously barred to women.

Sadly, Mary's promise as a scientist was cut off, and the manner of her death has long eclipsed her intellectual life. On a summer's day in 1869 she and her husband were invited for a ride in a steam-powered motor car, the invention of her cousin William's son. Near Birr, the driver took a bend too fast at three and half miles an hour, and Mary was thrown in front of the vehicle. The vehicle ran over her and she died instantly of a broken neck. She has gone down in history as the world's first fatality in a motor car accident.

AGNES MARY CLERKE

1842–1907

Astrophysics researcher and writer

'Year by year, details accumulate and the strain of keeping them
under mental command becomes heavier.'
Agnes Mary Clerke

The shy, self-taught workaholic Agnes Mary Clerke could have chosen the more conventional world of music to excel in because she was a gifted pianist, but instead she committed to exploring the mysterious world of science.

Born in Skibbereen, Co Cork, in 1842, Agnes and her siblings inherited a love of science from their father, John Clerke. He was a bank manager but also an astronomer. They inherited a love for music from their mother, Catherine Deasy. At the insistence of their parents the Clerke girls, Agnes and Ellen, were educated to a high level by the Ursuline nuns. By the age of eleven, Agnes had devoured a book named *Outlines of Astronomy*, by the pioneering astronomer William Herschel (1738–1822). By the age of fifteen, Agnes had already started the research for her own book about astronomy. She was hooked.

Agnes Mary Clerke, 1905.

When she was aged nineteen, Agnes's upwardly mobile family moved to Dublin. She had to stay at home and watch while her brother Aubrey attended Trinity College – as a woman in the 1860s, she was not permitted to go. He won a gold medal for his degree in mathematics, and another for experimental and natural science. However, her supportive sibling shared books with her and enabled her to study maths and astronomy at university level at home.

In the 1870s, the family tended to spend winters in Italy – Rome, Naples and Florence. Agnes and her older sister Ellen were being 'finished' and made fit for society. (Ellen was also a scientist and poet, who published astronomical monographs, a novel, a travel guide, and poems, and wrote in German and Italian, as well as in English.) Agnes practically lived in the public libraries, always studying her main subject, the history of astronomy. But she also became fluent in Italian and German, and she kept up her music. In fact, the composer Franz Liszt was complimentary about Agnes's piano-playing.

Agnes started her writing career in earnest in 1877, when the family relocated to London. She submitted articles for the *Edinburgh Review* on subjects ranging from Copernicus to the Mafia to the origin of diamonds. As it happened, the same publishers, A&C Black, were producing the

Encyclopaedia Britannica, and Agnes was asked to contribute a number of scientific biographies on Kepler, Galileo, Lavoisier and others.

In 1885, Agnes published her *Popular History of Astronomy*, the work that made her name. In it, she sets out to describe 'in simple language', as she wrote in a preface, the new discoveries happening in astronomy. She was as good as her word. Her style is clear and direct, and even today is easy to follow, unlike the writing of her more pompous contemporaries. On foot of this she was offered collaborative positions at the Royal Greenwich Observatory, but her courage failed her and she refused, which she later came to regret. She continued to work alone.

Her output was considerable. She published *The System of the Stars* (1890), *The Herschels and Modern Astronomy* (1895), *Problems in Astrophysics* (1903), and *Modern Cosmogonies* (1906). She also wrote non-scientific essays on the Classics and 159 biographies for the *Dictionary of National Biography*.

The Royal Institution awarded Agnes the Actonian Prize, which came with 100 guineas, in 1892. In 1903 she was made an honorary member of the Royal Astronomical Society. She was invited to speak at the Royal Society, but as a shy and retiring person, she found it onerous, claiming she 'had no liking for it, nor indeed was well-suited for it'.

According to *Oifig na bPaitinní* (Irish Patents Office), Agnes has had a crater on the moon named after her. The Clerke Crater is on the edge of the Sea of Serenity, near to the landing site of Apollo 12.

Immersed in intellectual pursuits to the last, Agnes was still writing astronomy entries for the *Encyclopaedia Britannica* when she came down with a bad cold. She died of pneumonia in London, in 1907, aged sixty-five.

DR DOROTHY STOPFORD PRICE

1890–1954

BCG pioneer

'There is no condition which demands correct diagnosis more
urgently than does primary tuberculosis in children
and adolescents.'
Dorothy Stopford Price, *Tuberculosis in Childhood* (1942)

Through her own efforts, this tenacious medical pioneer is largely responsible for saving hundreds if not thousands of lives.

Dorothy Stopford was one of four children born into a middle-class, professional family in Clonskeagh, Co Dublin. Dorothy's medical interests may have stemmed from her mother, Constance Kennedy, whose father, Evory Kennedy, had served as a master of the Rotunda Lying-in Hospital, a Dublin maternity hospital. Dorothy's own father, Jemmett Stopford, was a civil servant, and her aunt was the nationalist historian Alice Stopford Green.

After Jemmett's death from typhoid in 1902, Dorothy and her family had to leave their Dublin home for financial reasons. They relocated to

Dr Dorothy Stopford Price.

London, where Dorothy was educated at St Paul's School for Girls, still an élite establishment today. In 1915 she rejected a place at a London art college, and chose to return home to Dublin, to study medicine at Trinity.

Come the Easter Bank Holiday Monday of 1916, Dorothy was staying at one of the smartest addresses in Dublin, the Under-Secretary's Lodge at the Phoenix Park as a guest of the Under Secretary himself, old colonial hand Sir Matthew Nathan. The diary she kept over Easter Week provides a unusual perspective of the events. In it, she described how she could hear 'Sinn Féiner corner-boys and ne'er-do-wells' blowing things up, and how lenient the military were being with the rebels. Shockingly, she notes there are even 'women SFs about with guns'!

But when the executions started in early May, Dorothy was as horrified as the rest of the country. She rejected conventional politics and became a supporter of Sinn Féin.

Graduating as both doctor and midwife in 1921, during the War of Independence, Dorothy became a medical officer to the IRA, and treated wounded men who were on the run at her clinic in Kilbrittain, Co Cork. She also gave lectures in First Aid to Cumann na mBan. During the Civil War (1922–23), she supported the anti-Treaty side but, in the spirit of even-handedness, made her medical expertise available to police at the local RIC Barracks.

Dorothy moved back to Dublin in 1923, determined to make a difference to the health of the nation. The only senior medic who would consider giving her a job was her friend Dr Kathleen Lynn, whom she had known since Trinity days. Kathleen had founded St Ultan's Hospital for Infants in 1919. Dorothy worked there for the rest of her career.

In 1925 Dorothy married Liam Price, a district justice and antiquarian. She chose to join her maiden name with her husband's name to become Dr Stopford Price. The couple lived in Dublin's Fitzwilliam Square and had no children.

Ireland in the 1920s had been in the grip of 'the white plague', as TB was known, for many decades. Hardly a family – particularly a poor family – was untouched by its rampages. Dorothy realised there was very little immunity to TB in the Irish population and started investigations. A scheme to send infected slum children to 'sunshine homes' by the sea for holidays got her support. Meanwhile, she read foreign medical papers and analysed data.

For example, according to a contemporary report in *The Irish Independent*, in 1939, she made a speech highlighting the fact that Ireland had 'an adolescent population' which, although it had only 20–30 percent infection rate in the 15–25 age group, had one of the highest death rates in Europe. This was because initial infection was ignored and regarded as self-healing, whereas Dorothy's investigations showed that intervention was required at the moment of first infection with the *tubercle bacterium*. Before the advent of the Bacillus Calmette-Guérin (BCG) vaccination, the main intervention was bed-rest, which gave the immune system a chance to defeat the infection.

Dorothy researched the BCG. Today this vaccine is given to babies as a routine part of public health programmes in many developed-world countries, but in Dorothy's day it was highly controversial. She imported it from France, and by 1937, once convinced it was safe, tested her theory on her patients, making St Ultan's the first hospital in Ireland or Britain to provide the BCG. The improvement in the condition of the children was dramatic:

> During the past four years ... it has been possible in the Tuberculosis
> Department of St Ultan's hospital to reduce the mortality rate from
> tuberculosis in the 0–1 year period from 77 percent to 28 percent.
>
> DS Price, *Tuberculosis in Childhood* (1942), John Wright and Sons, Bristol

Eventually Dorothy became convinced that she could go further: a mass vaccination programme would save many lives and make a huge difference to the health of the nation.

Battling the aftermath of rheumatic fever herself, Dorothy spent the gruelling years of the 1940s battling with the Catholic Church to have an Anti-TB League established in the country, and campaigning for mass immunization. The objection from the Catholic hierarchy was that they believed it was the right and responsibility of parents, not the State, to provide healthcare for a child. In reality, this was fuelled by a disapproval of Dorothy and some of her non-Catholic colleagues, and the fact that the Church ran most of the healthcare practices and facilities of the nation – including anything to do with family planning – and were not about to relinquish control of any of it.

Eventually Dorothy was victorious. In 1949 she was made head of the national vaccination programme by Health Minister Noel Browne, who had had TB himself and had lost several close family members to the disease. Ireland was one of the last countries in Europe to have such a programme. Dorothy was nominated for World Health Organization (WHO) awards for her work.

Dorothy did not live to enjoy her success for long. She suffered a stroke in 1950, and died of a second stroke in 1954. She is buried in Tallaght.

PROFESSOR
SHEILA TINNEY
1918–2010

The first Irish-educated woman to receive a doctorate in the
mathematical sciences

*'[Sheila is the] best equipped and most successful of the younger
generation of theoretical physicists in this country.'*

Nobel Prizewinner Paul Dirac

Mathematics and music were in Sheila Tinney's blood. Sheila
Power, as she was born, was the daughter of Michael Power, the professor of mathematics at University College Galway and she absorbed alge-
bra, geometry, trigonometry and calculus throughout her childhood. But
this childhood ended dramatically for Sheila, aged just twelve, when her
mother Caroline, a gifted pianist, died tragically in childbirth. The legacy
she left her six children, including two sets of twins, was a lifelong passion
for music.

Sheila was sent to boarding school first in Galway and then in Dublin at
St Mary's Dominican Convent in Cabra, where in 1935 she got honours
in maths (one of only eight girls in Ireland to take it), and gained the
highest marks in the country in geometry and Latin. Already an academic

*Sheila Tinney, née Power, at a conference at the Dublin Institute
for Advanced Studies, 1942.*

high-flyer, Sheila graduated with a First in mathematical science in 1938
from University College Dublin (UCD). She came top of her class.

Like Dr Emily Winifred Dickson before her, after doing her Masters
at UCD, Sheila took a travelling scholarship from the National University
of Ireland (NUI). She chose to research crystal lattices and completed her
PhD in only two years at Edinburgh University in 1941. She is believed
to be the first Irish-educated woman to receive a doctorate in the mathematical sciences. She published her first paper, based on her thesis, in 1942.

Returning to Dublin in 1941, Sheila, then aged twenty-three, became an
assistant lecturer at UCD, and was also one of the first scholars appointed
to the brand new Dublin Institute for Advanced Studies (DIAS). She
developed an interest in quantum physics, and wrote papers with Edwin

Schrödinger, Hideki Yukawa, and Walter Heitler.

In 1948 Sheila took a sabbatical on a scholarship and became a visiting scholar at the Institute for Advanced Study in Princeton, New Jersey, where she knew Albert Einstein. On her return in 1949 she was one of a vanguard of just four women to be elected to the Royal Irish Academy. They were the first female members in the institution's 175-year history, and were admitted after the RIA lost a legal battle over accepting them.

Sheila married engineer, Sean Tinney, in 1952, and changed her professional surname from Power to Tinney. The couple had three gifted children. DIAS made her a research associate in theoretical physics in 1954. But, back at UCD, though she had been a staff lecturer since 1945, it took another twenty-one years before she was finally made an associate professor of mathematical physics in 1966 – somewhat longer than any of her male colleagues.

Sheila was known throughout her career, not only for her brilliant mind, but also her efforts to break down gender barriers for other Irish women scientists. She retired at the age of sixty, and pursued her love of music and sport until she fell prey to Alzheimer's disease, when she was in her eighties. She died in a nursing home in Dublin, aged ninety-two. In 2018 the Royal Irish Academy commemorated the 100th anniversary of her birth by participating in Women on Walls, an art project celebrating pioneering female academicians.

DID YOU KNOW?

*   *   *

Ellen Hutchins (1785–1815) of Ardnagashel, west Cork, was Ireland's first female botanist. She identified many new non-flowering species and was also an exceptional artist. There is an Ellen Hutchins Festival in her honour.

*   *   *

The first female member of The Royal Astronomical Society was **Annie Scott Dill Maunder** (1868–1947) from Strabane, Co Tyrone. There is a moon crater named after her.

*   *   *

Cork woman **Cynthia Evelyn Longfield** (1896–1991) was affectionately known as Madame Dragonfly because of her pioneering work as an entymologist. She became the first female president of the Natural History Society of London, and donated her life's works to the Royal Irish Academy, Dublin.

*   *   *

Two Irish nurses, **Mary Fleming** and **Aileen Turner**, were working in the TB ward of Grove Park Hospital, London, in 1941 when it was bombed. They climbed back into the building and rescued their trapped patients just before the building partly collapsed. They both received the George Medal for 'quickness, coolness and courage in rescuing seventeen patients from almost certain death'.

*   *   *

WORKING-CLASS HEROINES

'For these be the times that try men's souls – and women's.'

Winnie Carney

WINIFRED CARNEY

1887–1943

Trade unionist

'For these be the times that try men's souls – and women's.'

Winifred Carney in *The Irish Worker* (1913)

In the political turmoil of early twentieth-century Ireland, the personal courage and commitment of Winifred Carney inspired many women.

Marie Winifred 'Winnie' Carney was born of a 'mixed marriage' in Bangor, Co Down, and raised as a Catholic. After her father left the family to go and live in London, she, along with her mother and six siblings, moved to Belfast's Falls Road area.

Winnie received a good education in a Christian Brothers school. She learned to play the piano, and after leaving school she acquired typing and clerking skills, securing a job as a legal secretary. By 1900 Winnie had joined the local Gaelic League, where she came into contact with suffragism and socialism. She soon became interested in trade unionism.

In 1912 Winnie was asked to help with clerical work in the Irish Transport Workers' Union (ITWU). It was through this role that she met James Connolly, who was the General Secretary of the union. Winnie was impressed by Connolly – he talked a lot of sense about the 'rotten social system', which made men the slaves of capitalism, and women the slaves

Winnie's nationalism was inspired by her socialism.

of men, and he advocated revolution. Enormous trust grew between them in the course of their union work, and Winnie was privy to all Connolly's arrangements and plans for the future. To prepare herself, Winnie joined Cumann na mBan in 1914, so that when, in the fateful spring of 1916, Connolly asked Winnie if she would become his aide-de-camp (or right-hand woman) in Dublin for the expected uprising, Winnie readily agreed.

There is no extensive record left by the modest Winnie of her experiences in the GPO – hence the title of the biography by Helga Woggon, *Silent Radical* – but Winnie found herself at the very centre of the action in Easter Week.

Armed with a Corona typewriter and a Webley gun, Winnie spent Easter

Week moving from room to room in the beleaguered GPO, typing mobilisations, despatches and Commandant Connolly's orders. When Connolly was wounded she refused to leave him until forced to on 29 April when the rebels surrendered.

Waiting for sentencing in Kilmainham's cells, Winnie and the other women could hear their comrades being executed in the prison yard. Winnie's own sentence was light: eight months internment, which she spent in an English prison.

In post-Rising Ireland, Winnie's insistence on a workers' republic being as important as a free Ireland made her less popular than she might have been. In the 1918 general election, supported by Cumann na mBan whose president she had become, Winnie made a game but doomed attempt to run as a Sinn Féin candidate.

The flag commemorating the first anniversary of James Connolly's death hung at the front of the original Liberty Hall.

'I remain an extreme anarchist,' she wrote, 'because, you see, I too am determined I shall one day share the responsibility of directing the government of the country.' Unfortunately, in socially conservative Ireland, that day was slow to come.

During the Civil War, Winnie's home became a safe house for IRA on the run, including Countess Markievicz. She was hauled up several times by the authorities for membership of banned organisations, such as the Irish Republican Prisoners' Dependants' Fund. With the advent of the Free State government in 1922, Winnie became disillusioned, both with it and with the subsequent president Éamon de Valera. She went back to live in Belfast and concentrated her energies on labour activism.

Due to her membership of the Northern Ireland Labour Party in the mid-1920s, she became friends with one George McBride from Belfast's Shankill Road area. He seemed an unlikely suitor: Unionist, Protestant and a World War I British army veteran. In addition, he was nine years younger than Winnie. But they agreed on much more than they disagreed on (including radical reform of labour rights), and their marriage, which took place in a registry office in Holyhead (neither of them liked their own religion), was a famously happy one. Winnie's mother lived with them until her death.

Winnie was afflicted with ill health in later life.

Winnie gave up active membership of her branch of the ITGWU when she married and she scaled back her activities in the 1930s due to the increasing ill-health that was the legacy of the TB she had contracted as a youngster.

Winnie died, aged only fifty-five, and the heartbroken George never remarried. She was buried at Milltown Cemetery, Belfast. Her grave was completely overlooked by both local authorities and national governments, but in 1985, the National Graves Association, which maintains the graves of Irish republicans, finally gave 'the typist with the Webley' a headstone. It identifies her as a 'life-long republican socialist'. George is buried in a separate grave nearby.

ROSIE HACKETT

1893–1976

Rebel and trade unionist

'It took 400 police to take four women ...'
Rosie Hackett

A woman such as the diminutive but determined Rosie Hackett might have spent years being overlooked by history – but never by those she fought for, the ordinary people of Dublin, for whom she was, and still is, a working-class heroine.

Rosanna 'Rosie' Hackett was born in a tenement in central Dublin. After her father died and money became scarce, Rosie went to work first in a paper factory and then in the largest employer of women in Dublin, Jacob's Biscuit Factory. Here, according to the socialist leader James Connolly, the conditions were so bad they reduced workers' life expectancy by twenty years. It was here that the teenage Rosie became involved in the trade unionism that was to be the passion of her life. In 1911, she helped found the Irish Women Workers' Union (IWWU). It immediately gave women a voice in Jacob's and helped gain a long-overdue pay rise.

In the August of 1913, some 300 employers across Dublin had had enough of workers demanding decent working conditions; after all, it was affecting their profits. They systematically started to fire those with union

Members of the IWWU pose for a photograph. Rosie Hackett is in the front row, second from the left, next to Winnie Carney.

membership. This led to one of the biggest industrial actions in Ireland's history, the notorious Dublin Lockout. Over a period of six months, from late August, 20,000 workers were literally locked out of places of employment. By the end of September they and their families – some 100,000 people all together – were starving, and most were on the point of becoming homeless. The Lockout caused many violent clashes between police and workers, even resulting in deaths. One co-worker of Rosie's, a sixteen-year-old named Alice Brady, was shot by a scab worker and died two weeks later of her wounds.

Along with Constance Markievicz and others, Rosie helped set up soup kitchens for the starving in Liberty Hall, but the destitute strikers simply could not survive. The Lockout ended when employers were able to force workers to return to work on their terms. Jacob's Biscuit Factory refused to re-employ Rosie.

Rosie started clerking full-time for the union at Liberty Hall, and she learned printing, which was to be useful later. By now she was coming into contact with all the major agitators for change in Ireland, including James Connolly. It wasn't long before she joined his Irish Citizen Army to fight for Irish independence.

In the 1916 Easter Rising, the tiny figure of Rosie was to be seen in the thick of the fight at the St Stephen's Green/College of Surgeons garrison, as she helped the wounded. She was the only woman among a group of men that volunteered for the job of producing the 1916 Proclamation from an ancient printing press in the city.

After the surrender of the rebels, Rosie went to Kilmainham Jail for ten days. On her release she continued to work at Liberty Hall. When the first anniversary of the execution of James Connolly came around, Liberty Hall hung a banner up in commemoration. It said 'JAMES CONNOLLY MURDERED, May 12th 1916'. The police came and removed it immediately, but Rosie's response was to re-print the same banner. She and three other women, Helena Molony, Jinny Shanahan and Brigid Davis, raced to the top of the building, nailed the doors behind them and barricaded themselves in. They hung the banner across the front of the building from the roof, in clear view of everyone. Later Rosie said gleefully,

I always felt that it was worth it, to see all the trouble the police had in getting it down. No one was arrested. Of course, if it took 400 police to take four women, what would the newspapers say?

In the 1920s, Rosie joined Cumann na mBan and also continued with her trade union activities, particularly re-galvanizing the IWWU, which had at its height a membership of 70,000 women workers. She worked at Eden Quay co-operative for forty years, and she received a gold medal in 1970 to mark the sixty years she had been working in trade unionism.

When Rosie died, aged eighty-four, she was buried with military honours in Glasnevin Cemetery, Dublin. She was honoured in 2014 when Dublin voted that a new bridge near Liberty Hall be named after her. Although there is a bridge in Chapelizod called after the mythical spirit of the Liffey, Anna Livia, the Rosie Hackett Bridge is, so far, the only city centre bridge over the Liffey named after a real woman.

Plaque commemorating the opening of the Rosie Hackett Bridge, Dublin, 2014.

MARGARET SKINNIDER

1893–1971

Trade unionist and revolutionary

'Scotland is my home but Ireland is my country.'
Margaret Skinnider

Born in North Lanarkshire, Scotland, of Irish parents, Margaret spent childhood holidays in Monaghan and formed a strong attachment to her roots. It is said that as a twelve-year-old she read *The Story of Ireland for Young and Old* (1885) and it affected her deeply.

Education was important in the Skinnider household and Margaret did well at school. On leaving, she worked as a maths teacher in Glasgow, but read widely and remained concerned about the appalling living conditions for people in the north of Ireland. She wanted to change things.

Inspired by Countess Constance Markievicz, Margaret joined the Glasgow branch of Cumann na mBan; her interest was not purely nationalist, but socialist and feminist. In 1914, at the outbreak of World War I, she joined a local rifle club, which had been established to train people in the event of an invasion – a last defence of the British Empire. Margaret was amused at the irony of her situation: the British Empire was training

CONSTITUTION, CORUGHADH.

Cumann na mBan is an independent body of Irishwomen pledged to maintain the Irish Republic established on January 21st, 1919, and to organise and train the women of Ireland to work unceasingly for its international recognition. All women of Irish birth or descent are eligible for membership, except that no woman who is a member of the enemy organisation or who does not recognise the Government of the Republic as the lawfully constituted Government of the people can become a member.

OBJECTS :   **(Cuspora)**

    1. (*a*) The complete separation of Ireland from all foreign powers.
        (*b*) The Unity of Ireland.
        (*c*) The Gaelicisation of Ireland.

II.   **MEANS**.   **(Slighthe).**

    1. To maintain the Republic by every means in our power against all enemies, foreign and domestic.

    2. To assist Oglaigh na h-Eireann, the Irish Volunteers, in its fight to maintain the Republic.

    3. That at elections, Cumann na mBan, as such, give no assistance to any Organisation which does not give allegiance to the Government of the Republic.

    4. To become perfect citizens of a perfect Irish Nation by :—
        (*a*) Taking Honour, Truth, Courage and Temperance as the watchwords of Cumann na mBan ; (*b*) by fostering an Irish atmosphere, politically, economically and socially ; (*c*) discouraging Emigration by brightening the social life of the district ; (*d*) supporting Irish industries.

    5. At all times and in all places to uphold the spirit and the letter of the Cumann na mBan Constitution.

    6. The Constitution of Cumann na mBan may not be altered except by a two-third majority vote of a Convention.

The Cumann na mBan Constitution.

her to become a crack shot, but she would be using her skills to attempt to overthrow it in Ireland.

In the run-up to the Easter Rising of 1916, Margaret travelled between Glasgow and Dublin, sometimes smuggling bomb-making detonators in her hat. The week before the planned rebellion, Margaret became a courier for Connolly's ICA, and during the Rising itself she operated as a sniper, the only woman combatant in the GPO. She sustained three serious gunshot wounds while in action. When the general surrender was called, she was hospitalized at St Vincent's, under guard, for nearly two months. She was taken to Bridewell Prison, but released the same day on medical grounds. She went to Scotland to recover before returning to live in Ireland. Margaret was the only woman combatant wounded in the Rising.

In 1917 Cumann na mBan and the Glasgow Volunteers awarded Margaret the Irish Cross for her bravery. In that year too, Margaret published a book, *Doing My Bit For Ireland*, which described her early life and 1916 experiences. In it she describes how her commanding officer Michael Mallin was reluctant to let her be a sniper instead of a courier, but she insisted, saying:

> I say we have the same right to risk our lives as the men; that in the constitution of the Irish Republic, women and men are equal.
>
> *Doing My Bit For Ireland* (1917)

Margaret was active in Cumann na mBan during the War of Independence (1919–1921). When the Anglo-Irish Treaty was signed in London, she took the anti-Treaty side. In the ensuing Civil War in Ireland (1922–23), she was arrested and briefly imprisoned for possession of a weapon. At the

Women combatants in the Easter Rising were issued with a Webley gun or rifle.

request of Éamon de Valera, she went on a fundraising and lecturing tour to America.

At the close of the Civil War and the establishment of the Free State, Margaret started work as a teacher at a primary school in Dublin. She remained an ardent socialist and retained her interest in the condition of women workers, agitating for better pay and conditions for women in teaching.

In 1946 Margaret became a member of the executive body of the Irish National Teachers' Organisation (INTO) and was a member of the strike committee during the seven-month Dublin teachers' strike in that year. She fought particularly for the rights of women resulting in the introduction of common incremental salary scales for women and single men in 1949. In 1956 she became INTO's president. During her time heading up INTO Margaret represented Ireland at the World Conference of the Organisations of the Teaching Professions in the Philippines.

Margaret retired from teaching in 1961. In retirement she had to do battle once again – this time for her own pension rights as a combatant in 1916, which the Irish government had been reluctant to give a woman. In 1965–66, she sat on the Committee that advised on the 50th anniversary commemorations of the 1916 rising.

She died aged seventy-nine, after an active and productive life, and is buried in the Republican plot at Glasnevin, close to her inspiration, Countess Markievicz.

DID YOU KNOW?

* * *

Dublin woman **Teresa Mulally** (1728–1803) fulfilled her desire to educate poor girls because she won an eighteenth-century version of the Lotto. In the 1760s, educating Catholics was a crime punishable by death. But Teresa defied the Crown and secretly created a two-room school for girls, where she gave them a chance at an honest living by teaching them literacy, maths and needlework. The school opened at 8 am and closed at 6 pm, and students had to slip in and out one by one.

* * *

Second-generation Irish sisters **Mary Burns** (1821–63) and **Lizzie Burns** (1827–78) both lived with Friedrich Engels, co-author with Karl Marx of the *Communist Manifesto*, one of the most influential political works in history. They guided him through the Manchester Irish slums and influenced his work. Mary lived with him until her death; Lizzie married him on her own deathbed.

* * *

The first union of schoolteachers in the USA was founded by **Kate Kennedy** (1827–1890), from Gaskintown, Co Meath. After receiving lower wages than male colleagues, she campaigned for and won equal pay legislation, passed in 1874.

* * *

Helena Molony (1883-1967) was in the Irish Citizen Army, which attempted to take Dublin Castle during the Easter Rising. She was also an actress, who used to come offstage in the middle of a play at the Abbey theatre, rush to address meetings in her other role as political activist, and rush back in time for her next cue.

Born in Co Wexford, **Mary 'Pick Handle' Fitzgerald** (1885–1960) moved to South Africa as an adult and found work as a typist for the Mine Workers' Union. (It was open only to white workers; black African miners, who did most of the most dangerous work, did not have a union until 1919.) Versions of how she earned her nickname vary, but one common story claims that she rallied the striking miners, waving a pick handle as a weapon against the police. Johannesburg City Council named a square after her, considering her to be the first female trade unionist in South Africa.

Irish Citizen Army outside Liberty Hall, 1914.

VOTES!

'Votes for Women now! Damn your war!'

Irish Citizen (August 1914)

ANNA HASLAM
1829–1922

Pioneering feminist

'Sir, in December last the military authorities in Ireland
represented strongly the great prevalence of venereal disease
among the garrison of Dublin, and urged that the provisions of
the Contagious Diseases Acts should be extended to that City...
I have arranged with the Governors of the Westmoreland Lock
Hospital to offer additional accommodation to diseased women;
and I hope that this measure may have some result in improving
the health of the garrison.'
Marquis of Hartington, House of Commons Debate,
4 May 1883

Anna Maria Haslam, née Fisher, worked for women's rights for more than fifty years. She was able to vote for the first time in a national election in 1918, aged nearly ninety.

Anna was born into a Quaker family in Youghal, Co Cork, in 1829, the sixteenth of seventeen children. Her formative teenage years were dominated by the Great Famine of 1845–49. As Quakers, Anna's family had a long tradition of community service (as well as abolitionism, pacifism and equal rights), and she worked in soup kitchens for the starving, and in

Anna Haslam with her husband, Thomas.

employment initiatives set up for young women.

After the Famine, Anna left Ireland to complete her education in Yorkshire, England. While there she met a Co Laois man, a teacher named Thomas Haslam. The two were married in 1854 in a Cork registry office and moved to Dublin. It was the beginning of a radical campaigning partnership.

The Haslams had an interest in women's rights, reproductive rights and family planning. The couple decided against having children themselves, and chose celibacy as a method of birth control. Thomas went on to write a book advocating various forms of birth control – within marriage, of course – but this 'obscene' publication got him expelled from the Quakers. (Unfortunately for his readers, the advice he gave about natural contraception was so biologically inaccurate it probably resulted in many births.)

Anna took up the cause of women's rights in 1866 when she joined a petition to Parliament calling for votes for women. At this time the controversial and notorious Contagious Diseases Act was attempting to tackle sexually transmitted disease by focusing only on punishing women prostitutes, particularly in areas where there were army barracks. Prostitutes were forced to undergo examination and, if found to have contracted a sexually transmitted infection, they were interned for up to a year, while their male clients were not treated nor even interviewed. This was obvious injustice and Anna swung into a campaign against it, along with her Belfast-based friend and comrade Isabella Tod. The act was repealed in 1886, signalling the end of legalised prostitution.

In 1876 Anna and Thomas founded the Dublin Women's Suffrage Association (DWSA), a cross-party group peacefully demanding women's suffrage. It's important to note that Anna was a suffragist, not a suffragette. Later more militant suffragettes, such as Hanna Sheehy Skeffington, were in favour of direct actions, including violence, as a means to an end. In comparison, Anna's activities may even seem tame, confined as they were to holding meetings to raise awareness and writing to those in power such as MPs. But her actions were radical for the day and she was nothing if not tenacious. Her campaign was crushed time and again, notably in the 1884 Reform Act, which increased the franchise to allow more men of property to vote yet included nothing for women of similar standing. But the dogged Anna persisted; astonishingly, she attended and took minutes at every meeting from 1876 to 1913, when she resigned as secretary.

In the 1890s, Anna campaigned for the right of Irish women to be elected Poor Law Guardians, a very significant local government job. The Poor Law was the only benefits system available at the time, and its elected officers could deploy finances and other resources to the destitute. The victory in this led to women also being voted onto local councils. The DWSA could now change its name to the Irish Women's Suffrage and Local Government Association (IWSLGA). It was an important step in showing the absurdity of having women decide policy in local governments all over the country, yet not permitting them to vote for a national government.

By the beginning of the twentieth century, revolutionary social, political and labour reform was in the air. Anna had recruited younger, more radical women to her cause, such as the feminist Hanna Sheehy Skeffington, who joined the IWSLGA in 1903, and went on to found the Irish Women's

Franchise League. As life president of the IWSLGA, Anna kept abreast of the activities of her younger comrades as they forced the government to listen to their demands.

In February 1918 all women over thirty years old in Ireland and Britain were granted the right to vote, and in the General Election of December of that year Anna Haslam made her way to a voting booth in Dublin to complete a journey she had been on for fifty-two years. She was cheered on by a procession of women from all political persuasions and all generations.

Anna is largely forgotten today, but a bench in St Stephen's Green, Dublin, honours her and her husband for 'their long years of public service, chiefly devoted to the enfranchisement of women'.

Soup kitchen run by Cork quakers during the Great Famine.

EVA GORE-BOOTH

1870–1926

Feminist, labour activist and poet

'We meet beyond Earth's barred gate/Where all the
world's wild Rebels are.'
Eva Gore-Booth, from 'Comrades' in *The Egyptian Pillar*
(1907)

The Gore-Booths of Lissadell, Co Sligo, in many ways embodied the Anglo-Irish Ascendency. Eva Gore-Booth was born on the family estate. Her early life was classic Big House – servants inside and out, hunting and horse-riding, tea and dinner parties, trips abroad, and famous visitors such as WB Yeats. But there was a crucial difference: compared with most landlords Eva's father was unusually conscientious with his tenants. In the Sligo famine of 1879, the Gore-Booth family provided food, suspended rents, and created profitable work. A family story tells how Eva was stopped while giving away her own coat to a hungry little girl from the estate. Before she turned ten, Eva had a social conscience.

At twenty-four she travelled the world with her father, a former Arctic explorer, and in 1896 she was sent to Bordighera, Italy, for her chronic lung problems. It was here that Eva met Esther Roper, who would become her life partner. Esther, an intelligent young Englishwoman from a factory

Eva Gore-Booth (left) with her sister Constance, later Countess Markievicz,
c.1890s.

background, had pulled herself up by the bootstraps and gained a degree. She was already politically active in Manchester as secretary for the Society of Women's Suffrage. By 1897 Eva had moved to that city into Esther's small terraced house. By 1899, she was on the executive of the National Union of Women's Suffrage Societies. From 1899 until 1913, Eva and Esther together worked unceasingly for labour reform and women's rights. In 1902, Eva founded the Lancashire and Cheshire Women Textile and Other Workers' Representation Committee. Between them, they orga- nized female flower-sellers, circus performers, barmaids and coal workers, whose right to work was threatened by legislation. (In 1911 Eva herself worked as a pit brow lass to draw attention to their plight.) In 1904, Eva founded the Manchester and Salford Women's Trade and Labour Council, and published her first volume of poetry. By 1905, Esther had become sec- retary of the National Industrial and Professional Women's Suffrage Soci- ety, although by now both Eva and Esther were distancing themselves from the increasingly militant strategies of the Pankhursts' Women's Social and Political Union (WSPU).

It was Eva who is credited for inspiring her sister, Constance Markiev- icz, to become active in politics, when she encouraged Constance to start a women's franchise league locally in Sligo. Constance's fame would eventually go on to eclipse her sister's, as she became a leading political activist and the first woman ever to be elected to the House of Commons (she did not take her seat). However, while Constance's passionate nature espoused Irish inde- pendence primarily, Eva was always more committed to labour and women's rights, and pacifism. In 1908, the sisters campaigned for the Conservative candidate for the seat of Manchester Northwest, who was a supporter of women's suffrage against the anti-feminist Winston Churchill. Eva spoke passionately and convincingly from the roof of a carriage pulled by four horses, which was driven around the city by Constance. The voters loved the stunt, and to his astonishment, Churchill failed to win the seat.

Eva's lung problems worsened in 1913 and she and Esther escaped the smog of Manchester for the slightly less dense smog of London. There they founded *Urania*, a radical feminist magazine, which controversially celebrated same-sex love more than a century before Ireland endorsed same-sex marriage by popular vote.

With the outbreak of war the following year, Eva and Esther became more active as pacifists, joining the Women's Peace Crusade. There was a major split between Irish and British feminists at this time: the Irish movement opposed conscription and Irish involvement in the war, but the pro-Empire British movement promoted conscription and suspended their suffrage campaign for the duration of the war.

Eva supported her sister's revolutionary activities from across the Irish Sea, but as a pacifist, she could never have taken an active role in the Easter Rising. After Constance was jailed in 1916 for her part, and her comrades began to be executed day by day, Eva went to Dublin Castle to plead for her sister's life. Constance's death sentence was commuted to life imprisonment (apparently because of her sex), and she was released the following year under a general amnesty. Back in London, Eva attended the trial of Sir Roger Casement, who was hanged for his part in the Rising. Afterwards she campaigned against capital punishment.

Eva spent the final ten years of her life writing poetry. In one, 'The Anti-Suffragist', she sees the world without female suffrage as a prison:

The princess in her world-old tower pined

A prisoner, brazen-caged, without a gleam

Of sunlight, or a windowful of wind;

She lived but in a long lamp-lighted dream.

They brought her forth at last when she was old;

The sunlight on her blanched hair was shed

Too late to turn its silver into gold.

"Ah, shield me from this brazen glare!" she said.

Eva died in 1926. Her partner Esther edited and published *The Poems of Eva Gore-Booth* (1929) and *The Prison Letters of Countess Markievicz* (1934), and lived until 1938. Eva and Esther are buried together in Hampstead, London.

GRETTA COUSINS
1878–1954

Suffragist, educationist and civil rights activist

'We women were convinced that anything which improved the
status of women would improve, not hinder, the coming
of real national self-government.'
Gretta Cousins, *We Two Together* (1950)

argaret 'Gretta' Gillespie was an exceptional lifelong cam-
paigner, who served prison sentences in three different countries for her
work in women's rights and national independence.

Gretta was born in Boyle, Co Roscommon, in 1878, the daughter of a
law clerk. She and her fourteen younger siblings came from a reasonably
affluent Unionist and Methodist background. Margaret studied on a scholarship at a girls' school in Derry and later at the Royal Academy of Music
in Dublin. She graduated with a Bachelor of Music degree from the RUI
in 1902. She married her soulmate, the poet and literary critic James Cousins the following year and, like him, became a vegetarian (a highly unusual
lifestyle choice for the times). The couple lived in Sandymount, Dublin,
where they played a full part in middle-class social life, hosting guests such
as James Joyce and WB Yeats.

As a witness to what she saw as her mother's economic servitude to her father, and a believer in women's economic independence, Gretta continued working as a music teacher after her marriage, but she was ready for more. She joined the Irish Women's Suffrage and Local Government Association (founded by Anna Haslam, see p93), and became its treasurer. In 1908 she and James co-founded the more militant suffragette group the Irish Women's Franchise League (IWFL) along with Hanna Sheehy Skeffington and her husband Francis. The purpose of the IWFL was to get women the vote, and Gretta was an active member, addressing public meetings (which she rehearsed for by practising in a field containing an attentive donkey) and regularly contributing to the IWFL's weekly newspaper *The Irish Citizen*. Meanwhile, Gretta and James became involved with Theosophy, a combination of Eastern and Western religious traditions, which they would follow for the rest of their lives.

James was almost as much of a feminist as Gretta, and it was he who made links with Emmeline Pankhurst's Women's Social and Political Union (WSPU) in London. In 1909, Gretta learned tactics from the WSPU, which she shared with the IWFL, such as pavement slogan-writing and running mass public meetings. In 1910 Gretta was one of the six Irish women invited to attend the 'Parliament of Women' at Caxton Hall, London. She ended up serving a month in Holloway Prison on that trip, for throwing stones at the windows of 10 Downing Street, the home of the British Prime Minister.

Actions as militant as this were becoming a necessity. Women – and particularly Irish women – were struggling to be heard. Irish people had no representation in their own country, so they had to confront the Westminster Parliament either directly or through the Irish Party, which sat at Westminster as a constitutional reform party, pushing for Home Rule. Gretta and her colleagues tried in vain to convince them to put a women's suffrage amendment in any Home Rule Bill for Ireland. But some Irish Party politicians felt that such a radical idea might not only jeopardize the whole question of getting Home Rule through Parliament, but be wholly an evil thing. John Dillon, Irish Party MP, was very clear about this in a letter to Hanna Sheehy Skeffington:

> Women's suffrage will, I believe, be the ruin of our Western civilisation.
> It will destroy the home, challenging the headship of man, laid down by
> God. It may come in your time – I hope not in mine.

But the Votes for Women movement was gaining momentum, and by 1912 the membership of the IWFL numbered a thousand, making it Ireland's largest suffrage society. In the summer of that year, Gretta and Hanna smashed windows at Dublin Castle, the centre of the British administration in Ireland. They each got a month in Tullamore Jail, Co Offaly, during which they went on hunger strike.

Gretta wrote:

> I am not a criminal but a political prisoner. My motives were neither
> criminal nor personal – being wholly associated with the agitation to
> obtain Votes for Women. I shall fight in every way in my power against
> being branded a criminal.

Gretta and Hanna got their way; they were granted political prisoner status.

From left, Meg Connery, Mabel Purser, Barbara Hoskins and Gretta Cousins on their release from Tullamore Jail, 1912.

In 1913 Gretta and James moved to Liverpool, England, where James had found work in a vegetarian food factory. Gretta's interests remained varied. She continued her feminist work with Pankhurst's WSPU, and making links between it and the IWFL back in Ireland. She became president of the Liverpool Vegetarian Society and founded a short-lived church specifically for women.

Mysticism was in the air in the early years of the twentieth century. In Dublin Gretta had been friendly with WB Yeats and discussed spirituality and clairvoyance with him, and even indulged in séances with a number of literary types. It wasn't just the spiritual appeal: Theosophy had a completely fresh approach to issues of gender and race. All were equal in the eyes of Theosophy.

Gretta had known leading Theosophist Annie Besant since 1906, and in 1915 Besant persuaded the Cousins to move to India.

Gretta became a teacher again – in English at a college this time rather than music in school, and she dedicated her spare time first to Indian feminism and then to women's education and Indian independence. Her experience in the Irish and English suffrage movements was useful, especially when she had to speak to the British, petition politicians, organize, lecture, and produce a journal. In 1916, she became the first non-Indian member of the Indian Women's University at Poona. In 1917 she co-founded the Women's Indian Association with Annie Besant and Dorothy Jinarajadasa. Their campaign worked to abolish child marriage, and promote education for girls and women. In 1917 Madras became the first Indian region to grant women full suffrage rights, a year before suffrage was granted in Ireland.

Gretta was horrified that for every ten boys' schools there was only one for girls. In 1919–20 she founded and acted as Head Teacher of the National Girls' School at Mangalore. In 1922, she became the first honorary woman magistrate in Madras, and in the same year published *The Awakening of Asian Womanhood* (1922).

In 1927 Gretta helped organise the All-India Women's Conference (serving as its president in 1937), which today still works towards the empowerment and education of women.

Along with Indian colleagues, Gretta helped organize the first All-Asia Women's Conference at Lahore, in what is now Pakistan, in 1931. The conference set a standard for pan-Asian feminism, focussing on common issues, such as political suffrage, property rights, and women and children's healthcare.

In 1932, Gretta travelled to New York and addressed a mass meeting to promote the Indian National Congress to protest imprisonment of lawyer Mohandas, later known as Mahatma, Gandhi. She also visited the League of Nations to speak for Indian independence. Back in India, Gretta was jailed for the third and final time in 1932, when she was fifty-four years old. She had contravened British-imposed conditions about speaking to mass meetings in Madras and she was imprisoned in Vellore jail for ten months.

Gretta was as energetic as ever when she emerged from prison. She continued to lecture and campaign for educational reforms and added justice for women in prison to her causes. Books she published in this period include *The Music of Orient and Occident: Essays Towards Mutual Understanding* (1935) and *Indian Womanhood Today* (1941). She and James wrote their joint biography, *We Two Together* (published 1950), rather sweetly taking alternate chapters.

In the 1940s Gretta suffered several very debilitating strokes. Her faithful partner James cared for her and she lived long enough to see Indian independence in 1947. The new Indian government recognised the four decades of hers and James's Indian work by giving them a much-needed government pension. Gretta died in Adyar, Chennai, India, in 1954, followed by James two years later.

DID YOU KNOW?

* * *

Dublin-born **Frances Power Cobbe** (1822–1904) was a progressive thinker who focussed extensively on domestic abuse. Her 1878 pamphlet, *The Truth on Wife Torture*, inspired a bill in Parliament that, for the first time, allowed wives legally to live apart from violent husbands.

* * *

Anne Jellicoe (1823–1880) of Co Laois founded Alexandra College, the first Irish college to offer women further education, which some of the women in this book attended. She also founded the first institute for women's employment in Ireland, known as the Queen's Institute.

* * *

Second-generation Irishwoman **Evelyn Gleeson** (1855–1944) knew the Yeats sisters in London and was inspired to finance Dun Emer, an Irish craft guild, based in Dublin. The idea behind it was to provide employment for local women to work on embroidery, printing and tapestry – all inspired by Irish stories and symbols.

* * *

Feminist **Jenny Wyse Power** (1858–1941) of Wicklow was active politically from Parnell's Land League to de Valera's constitution. She was the first president of Cumann na mBan, and a senator in the Irish Free State. The Proclamation of the Republic read out at the GPO during the Easter Rising was composed and signed at her home at 21 Henry Street, Dublin.

* * *

WOMEN OF FAITH

'Irish born, African reared.'

'A Tribute to Mother Kevin' by the Franciscan

Missionary Sisters for Africa

SAINT ITA

*c.*488–*c.*570

Poet and teacher

'Though they come my friendship craving
Sons of princes and of kings,
Not from them my soul finds saving
But to tiny Jesu clings.'

'St Ita's Fosterling', translated by Robin Flower

Although early Irish history is mainly populated with male chieftains and saints, through the mists of time – a placename here, an ancient reference there – some women's stories survive. Saint Ita is one such. Originally named Deirdre, Ita (in Irish Íde) was born near Drum in Co Waterford, a member of a local royal family. She was descended from a line of lawgivers, known as Brehons, and she is the best-known female Irish saint after St Brigid.

When it came time for Ita to marry, she rebelled. She fasted – an age-old method of obtaining justice by a subordinate on his or her masters – until she was allowed to enter a religious community instead. She changed her name to Ita, meaning 'thirst' (for goodness and knowledge of God).

Ita moved to present-day Killeedy (*Cill Íde*, or church of Íde) in Co Limerick, which became known after her. She founded a religious community there. Most religious houses were mixed, but Ita chose to found her convent exclusively for holy women.

Ita's poem is just one example of how she was seen in a motherly light: she founded a foster home/school for boys, and was the foster mother and teacher of Saint Brendan the Navigator, Saint Cummian, and Saint Mochaemóg. She was also credited with taking on the illegitimate child of one of her young nuns and rearing the baby as her own daughter. Her fame for charity and asceticism spread to the Continent, and her name appears in works scribed by French monks in the early ninth century for the Holy Roman Emperor, Charlemagne.

Tradition maintains that Ita authored the passionate poem *Isucán*, or *Jesukin*. In it she expresses her love for the infant Jesus as that of a nursing mother's love for her baby (while giving worldly clerics a swipe at the same time). Here it is in translation:

Babe Jesu lying
On my little pallet lonely
Rich monks woo me to deny thee
All things lie, save Jesu only.

Tiny fosterling I love thee
Of no churlish house thou art
Thou with angel wings above thee
Nestlest night-long next my heart.

Stained-glass window featuring Saint Ita, Church of Our Lady and Saint Kieran, Ballylooby, Co Tipperary.

Jesu thou angelic blossom
No ill-minded monk are thou;
child of Hebrew Mary's bosom,
In my cell thou slumberest now.

Though they come my friendship craving
Sons of princes and of kings,
Not from them my soul finds saving
But to tiny Jesu clings.

Virgins, sing your tuneful numbers
Pay your little tribute so;
On my breast babe Jesu slumbers
Yet in Heaven his soft feet go.

'Saint Ita's Fosterling', a ninth-century version,
translated by Robin Flower (1931)

Like St Gobnait, Ita's name is still popular in the province of Munster for baby girls, and her feast day of 15 January is celebrated particularly in west Limerick. In Ballylooby in Co Tipperary, a church dedicated to Our Lady and St Kieran contains a beautiful stained-glass image of St Ita. She is thought to be buried in Killeedy.

SISTER ANTHONY O'CONNELL

1814–1897

Army nurse

'Her work for humanity was spread over a long series of years and the heroic labours she performed were but one episode, but it was one that deserves to be handed down to history.'

George Barton, *Angels of the Battlefield* (1897)

This courageous nun was famous in her own lifetime for her nursing adventures during the American Civil War (1861–1865), when she treated both Union and Confederate soldiers alike.

Mary O'Connell was born in Limerick and, aged seven, emigrated to America with her whole family. Like so many Irish families, the O'Connells stayed in Boston initially but moved to Massachussetts state for work reasons.

Mary was educated by nuns and, when she was just twenty-one, joined a modern order of nuns founded by an American, St Elizabeth Seton. They were the Sisters of Charity, America's first home-grown Catholic religious order for women, and from then on Mary was known as Sr Anthony.

Sr Anthony moved to a convent in Cincinnati, Ohio, and her pre-Civil

Sister Anthony O'Connell.

War career focussed on looking after orphaned boys and running a combined school and orphanage. But there was a desperate need for trained nurses, and she joined the nursing sisters in a new hospital, St John's (known as Good Samaritan Hospital from 1866, and still serving the community today). By the time Civil War broke out some ten years later, she was running the hospital.

Sr Anthony's order attached themselves to the Union army as nurses. Today we might call them 'embedded'. As the bugle sounded for action and the soldiers marched away, Sr Anthony and her group of nuns followed, setting up field hospitals for the wounded alongside battlefields from Maryland to Kentucky to Tennessee. The Sisters of Charity were not alone; other orders that aided the wounded included the Sisters of Mercy, the Sisters of St Joseph, and the Sisters of the Holy Cross. The *Catholic Telegraph* of 8 June 1861, in an appeal for a horse and light wagon for the sisters, reported that, at one point, there were only seven Sisters of Charity engaged in the care of 12,000 men at Camp Dennison.

In his 1897 book *Angels of the Battlefield*, George Barton devotes a whole chapter to Sr Anthony and her actions in the famous Battle of Shiloh. She frequently braved the battlefield herself to bring in sick and dying soldiers, and she is credited with developing the first version of battlefield triage, a system of treating large groups of patients in order of urgency. It is worth remembering that in the days before anaesthetics and antibiotics, the nuns' main treatments consisted of dressing wounds, administering 'cordials', and keeping the bedbound as clean as possible. In the larger battles such as Gettysburg, Lynchburg, Richmond and Shiloh, there was often only one nun to care for up to a hundred wounded soldiers.

Sr Anthony and her sisters had been highly trained and were by now extremely experienced. She was well known for preventing amputations, which was by far the most common battlefield surgery performed in order to prevent gangrene and death. By using delicate medical care methods instead, such as splinting wounds and debriding (removing) dead or damaged flesh, she saved the limbs of dozens, if not hundreds, of soldiers. 'Let me see what I can do with this mangled member,' one story claims she shouted as she shooed the surgeons and their bone-saws away.

Sr Anthony comforted and helped desperate parents looking for their sons. On one occasion, after the Battle of Shiloh in 1862, she made the link between a father and his son, who had had part of his face shot away and was totally unrecognisable. She managed to reunite the pair and was able to report joyfully that 'he took his darling with him back to his home.'

Those wounded soldiers that were well enough to travel were transferred to Cincinnati. When transferring the wounded, which was mainly done by 'floating hospitals' as they were known, or steamboats, there were many dangers, with the nuns and dozens of crippled soldiers enduring bombardment and the ever-present risk of fire on board. Sr Anthony wrote how she and her sisters 'were often obliged to move further up the river, being unable to bear the stench from the bodies of the dead on the battlefield.'

Sr Anthony and her nuns, along with the other orders, were 'like violets blooming on a hidden place', according to the *Nashville Daily Union* of 3 November 1863. President Lincoln called the intrepid women 'veritable angels of mercy'. After the war, Sr Anthony's life was filled with the duties of her calling. She did well in convent elections and was repeatedly elected Procuratrix (responsible for purchases and invoicing). In 1878, she came out of retirement one final time to lead her nurses in tending the sick through America's worst-ever epidemic of the dreaded Yellow Fever. She died on 8 December 1897, her eighty-third birthday.

The former St Joseph Infant Home or Infant Asylum where Sr Anthony worked is now St Joseph Home, a residential facility for children and adults with mental and physical disabilities.

MOTHER KEVIN KEARNEY

1875–1957

Missionary

'Irish born, African reared.'

The Franciscan Missionary Sisters for Africa,

A Tribute to Mother Kevin (2018)

Mary Teresa Kearney was born in Knockenrahan, Arklow, Co Wicklow, the third and youngest daughter of Michael and Teresa Kearney, farmers. Her father died in an accident three months before her birth, and when she was just ten, her mother died. She was then reared by Granny Grennell, her maternal grandmother, in Curranstown, Arklow.

Teresa attended a local convent school in Arklow and in 1889 went to the Convent of Mercy at Rathdrum, where she trained as an assistant teacher. In 1893 she rejected a marriage proposal and moved to England to teach at a school run by the Sisters of Charity in Essex.

One night Teresa had a vivid dream of working in Africa, and the decision she'd been turning over was made. She entered the Franciscan Missionary Sisters of the Five Wounds at St Mary's Abbey, north of London, in 1895. She was professed in 1898 and took the name of Sister

Mary Kevin of the Sacred Passion, to be known as Sr Kevin.

In 1903, Kevin set off with five sisters, a bishop and several priests to follow her dream of establishing a mission in Nsambya, Uganda. The arduous African leg of the journey took eight days. The sisters hung off the sides of a train on the 'lunatic line' from Mombasa to Kisumu, Kenya, then sailed across the vast waters of Lake Victoria to reach Uganda. A seven-mile hike finished the adventure. The sisters' diary records:

> By this time we were exhausted and walking became a labour. Sister Kevin's face was burned brick-red, but she kept cheerful, and valiantly encouraged us all. We reached Nsambya drenched in sweat, caked with red dust; our heads ached and our eyes smarted; the world was whirling around us. Here again we were given a rousing welcome.
>
> *Love Is The Answer: The Story of Mother Kevin OSF* (1964),
>
> Sr M Louis OSF

Upon their arrival, the sisters immediately established a mission dispensary and school among the Baganda people. The Baganda were the largest ethnic group in what is now Uganda, and they had a sophisticated culture of their own before the colonizers came. Evangelizing them was one way that British colonizers maintained control —as far as they were concerned any Christian influence was better than Islamic influence. The weight of the British Empire in the region certainly would have aided Kevin and her colleagues, even though her own motives were spiritual rather than imperialistic.

By 1913 the sisters had expanded to three missions, which encompassed

Mama Kevina.

both medical and educational work. Kevin assumed leadership over them, taking the title Mother Kevin.

During World War I, Mother Kevin noticed that the Native Carrier Corps, the porters for European troops, were not as well treated as their white comrades, and she insisted that she oversee their treatment herself at Nsambya. According to www.catholicireland.net, her war work was recognised when King George V awarded her an MBE in 1918.

In 1920, back in Ireland, she trained in midwifery but wasn't allowed to qualify by the Catholic hierarchy who thought it was inappropriate for a nun. She spent many years battling this nonsensical prohibition. In the meantime, she persuaded a young Irish doctor called Evelyn Connolly to come out to Africa and train lay nurses, midwives, and doctors. Dr Connolly eventually became a Franciscan sister.

In 1923 Mother Kevin oversaw the foundation of an African congregation, the Little Sisters of St Francis, when several African girls approached her and asked to enter the religious life. The Little Sisters were to be, in her vision, African women, working for Africa. Her ideal was to hand over missions, schools and hospitals to them and move on.

Over the next thirty years Mama Kevina, as she was now called by most people, expanded the mission throughout Uganda, Kenya, Zambia and South Africa, opening one after another of primary, secondary, teacher-training and nursing schools. Often the schools would begin life under a tree, and then, with local support, a classroom would be built.

Additionally, the sisters cared for the outcasts of society, such as the blind and orphans. Mother Kevin opened two leprosaria, one of which was on the shores of Lake Victoria, where people suffering from leprosy and excluded from their own communities could live semi-independently by farming.

One of her major pre-occupations was with promoting education for African women. She understood that educating women showed a beneficial effect over just one or two generations, and was essential to reducing infant mortality, increasing life expectancy, and creating the ability to take over when she had moved on. She focussed all the educational resources she could on girls.

Despite the addition of the Little Sisters to aid the missionary effort, a chronic shortage of missionaries remained, and in 1928 Mother Kevin sought permission to establish a separate novitiate in England exclusively for the training of sisters for the African missions. She visited England in September 1928 to pursue this goal and the novitiate, connected with the original order at St Mary's Abbey, was opened in 1929 at Holme Hall in Yorkshire. The novitiate was so successful that in 1952 it separated from St Mary's Abbey and became an independent congregation, the Franciscan Missionary Sisters for Africa. The motherhouse was in Dundalk, with Mother Kevin as its superior-general. She continued in this office until she retired in 1955, aged eighty.

Mother Kevin remained active, and she raised funds in the United States, where the sisters had a convent near Boston, Massachusetts. She remained there until her death, aged eighty-two. Her remains were flown back to to Ireland, but upon hearing of her death, Ugandan Catholics called for their 'flame in the bush' to be returned to Uganda. She was flown over and buried in the cemetery at Nkokonjeru, the motherhouse of the Little Sisters of St Francis, where a hospital has developed from one of Mama Kevina's clinics. There is a postgrad medical college named in her honour in Nsambya, Uganda.

The influence of her fifty-four years as a missionary is reflected in the use of the word 'Kevina', which in parts of Uganda means any hospital, charitable institute, or indeed charitable action.

SISTER SARAH CLARKE

1919–2002

The Joan of Arc of British prisons

'I was sick and in prison and you visited me.'
Matthew 25:37

A nationalist nun, an artistic activist, an outspoken outsider – Sister Sarah Clarke might have been all these things, but she is best known for her dogged tenacity in the campaign to free seventeen people who were victims of miscarriages of British justice, in the cases of the Guildford Four, the Maguire Seven and the Birmingham Six.

Sarah was born in Eyrecourt, Co Galway, where her mother and father ran a pub, shop and farm. She was educated by nuns and decided early in life to follow a religious vocation. She joined the teaching order La Sainte Union in Killashee, Co Kildare, as a teenager; her name in religion was Sister Mary Auxilus. After teaching jobs in Athlone, and later in Sussex and Devon, Sarah taught at the La Sainte Union girls' school in Highgate, London, and studied art in her spare time. It was here in 1970 that this unassuming middle-aged nun had a epiphany – not religious, but political.

Northern Ireland in the late 1960s and early 1970s was suffering. There was massive discrimination against Catholics in the region in jobs, education and housing, and a civil rights movement was demanding equality. In 1970 Sarah got involved in the Northern Ireland Civil Rights Association (NICRA). She watched in horror as the nationalist and unionist communities tore each other apart, and bloody event followed bloody event. Bombings, shootings, kidnaps, reprisals became almost a weekly occurence. And over it all were two governments that at best refused to admit there was a war going on, and at worst colluded with terrorists during its progress.

In 1973 the war came to London with the Scotland Yard and Old Bailey bombings. Sarah identified with Irish prisoners – at first the guilty, then later the innocent – who had been jailed, and tried to ease their passage through the system. 'I was sick and in prison and you visited me,' Jesus had said, and this was her first and most basic impulse.

When the IRA took the bombing campaign to England, they killed scores and maimed hundreds of civilians in raids on pubs and clubs. After the bombings in Woolwich, Guildford, and Birmingham in 1974, which killed twenty-eight people, the Prevention of Terrorism Act was introduced by the government.

'Everything about the PTA was excessive,' Sarah was to write later in her autobiography. The Act jailed Irish people in Britain, and those visiting them, almost indiscriminately, creating fear in the community. People were reported to the police for listening to Irish music or speaking with an Irish accent. Holiday-makers from Ireland were arrested and held until they missed planes and ferries home. Working men and women were suddenly deported from Britain, with no reason given. One Irish woman reported her depressed husband missing. She was held for several days under the

PTA, until his body was discovered floating in the Thames. He had committed suicide.

It was under the PTA that a number of men and women – many from the same family – were rounded up, charged and convicted either of the bombings themselves or of handling explosives. The Guildford Four and Birmingham Six were all sentenced to life imprisonment in 1975. The Maguire Seven received long sentences in 1976 for handling explosives. The trouble was, none of them were guilty of the bombings. The police had extracted their confessions in dubious circumstances.

Convinced of the innocence of these seventeen people, Sarah wrote to establishment figures, both Conservative and Labour MPs, and the Church, about their case. She visited them regularly in prison and arranged their families' travel and accommodation during their own visits. One of the prisoners named her 'the Joan of Arc of the prisons'.

Sarah took a special interest in the plight of one prisoner, a man named Giuseppe Conlon. Giuseppe had hurried from Belfast to London when he heard his son Gerry was in prison under interrogation for the bombings. But instead of being able to help his son, he himself was arrested and convicted along with the rest of the Maguire Seven. Despite being seriously ill, Giuseppe got a twelve-year sentence, long enough to ensure he would die in prison, which he did in 1980, claiming his innocence until his last breath. His long-denied appeal for parole was granted the next day.

After years of campaigning, with the final admission of crucial evidence, and the fall from grace of several police officers, the convictions of all the surviving prisoners were overturned in 1991 and they walked free after more than sixteen years. The Prime Minister Tony Blair later issued an apology to them. No one else has yet been convicted of the bombings, which were claimed by an IRA unit in 2014.

For the rest of her life Sarah ministered to prisoners, concentrating on repatriating back to Ireland the elderly or ill, so they could be visited by family. Her 1995 autobiography damningly entitled *No Faith in the System* is dedicated to 'Giuseppe Conlon and the courageous, loyal families who were an inspiration to me and to others'. She died aged eighty-two and is buried with her family in Galway.

Sr Sarah was a focus of help and communication for the visiting families of prisoners.

DID YOU KNOW?

* * *

Born somewhere in western Britain or France in the fifth century, **St Dererca** was said to be the sister of St Patrick, and became known as the Mother of Saints. It is said she had seventeen sons, all of whom became bishops. Several of the bishops became saints, and one of them became the King of Brittany.

* * *

The popular Munster saint, **Gobnait**, who is especially associated with Muskerry, Co Cork, was actually born in north Clare in the sixth century. She is said to have miraculously repelled an army with a swarm of bees and, for many centuries, her beehive was kept as an object of veneration.

* * *

Carlow-born **Sr Mary Agatha O'Brien** was one of seven Sisters of Mercy who left Ireland for the Wild West in 1843. She led a small group to the fledgling city of Chicago in 1847 where she co-founded four schools, an orphanage and the city's first hospital, known as the Mercy. She died of exhaustion in her mid-thirties.

St Gobnait's window by Harry Clarke, Honan Chapel, Cork city.

Evangelist **Laura Thistlethwayte** née Bell (1894–1829) went from selling her body to saving her soul. Originally from Newry, Co Down, Laura was a teenaged prostitute in Dublin and London when she met and married a rakish English captain by the name of Thistlethwayte. The two led a rich, riotous life in London – and then Laura converted to evangelical Christianity. For thirty years, she was a lay preacher and became a close friend of Prime Minister William Gladstone, whose hobby of rescuing fallen women she shared.

Margaret Elizabeth Noble (1867–1911) from Dungannon, Co Tyrone, was working as a teacher when she heard a spiritual call that drew her to India. There she became a highly respected Hindu religious sister named Nivedita, who worked for women's education and Indian pan-nationalism.

The unusually titled **Dr Sr Mona Tyndall** (1921–2000), was both a missionary and a medical doctor. Cavan-born Mona was a Missionary Sister of the Holy Rosary (MSHR), and graduated from UCD in medicine. She set up mother-and-baby clinics in Nigeria and worked through the Biafran War, until she was imprisoned and deported. She retired to Cavan and was instrumental in forming the Irish government's foreign aid policy.

ACROSS THE SEA

'Oh brave Kate Shelley! Though hard toil thy daily portion be,
Mothers, with happy pride, now name their
daughters after thee ...'
The Daily Cairo Bulletin (1881)

NELLIE CASHMAN
1845–1925

Prospector and 'Angel of the Mining Camps'

'Her frank manner, her self-reliant spirit, and her emphatic and
fascinating Celtic brogue … indicated that she was a woman of
strong character and marked individuality.'
Arizona Weekly Star obituary (1925)

Ellen 'Nellie' Cashman (some say the name was an anglicisation of O'Kissane) worked the rough, tough territories of the Wild West and became 'the only woman mining expert in the United States' (*Tombstone Prospector*, 1897).

She was born in Midleton, Co Cork, in the first year of Ireland's Great Famine. The family struggled through unimaginable suffering, and when her father died around 1850, Nellie's mother was left with no support. She emigrated to Boston with Nellie and her younger sister Fanny.

When Nellie was around twenty the family went west to San Francisco, and Nellie got a job as bellhop, or elevator operator, in a large department store. It was here that Nellie was bitten by the mining bug. While her sister Fanny married an Irishman in San Francisco and had five children, Nellie and her mother headed to Nevada.

Nellie made herself at home in the silver- and gold-mining camps of the Wild West. She funded herself by running miners' hostels wherever she went – Nevada, Arizona, California. The wittily entitled *Tombstone Epitaph* of 1886 was one of many newspapers that advertised her boarding house, which charged 25 cents for meals and $6 per week for board – in advance, of course.

All the settlements she lived in were tough and full of brothels, but Nellie resolutely stayed out of the sex trade. A devout Catholic, she instead became known for her donations to local charities – and her nose for the next mining boom. She used her savings to 'grubstake' (fund) miners' expeditions, if she thought they were on to a good thing. It wasn't long before she went on her own expeditions.

In 1874, Nellie heard a rumour and travelled north with some miners to the Cassiar Mountains in British Columbia, Canada. It was here she had the experience that made her famous. Having made enough profit from the gold she mined in the mountains, she was comfortably wintering on the coast when she heard that a group of at least twenty-five miners, who had chosen to stay in the mountain camp, had been cut off by snow. They were sickening with scurvy and had few supplies left. Death seemed certain. Nellie responded by gathering supplies and equipment, and leading an expedition back to the miners. Some reports say the Canadian Army tried to stop her but she refused to go back until she found them. After this exploit, the name of Nellie Cashman became known to miners everywhere.

Nellie contributed to the building of churches, hospitals, and schools throughout her career, particularly for the Sisters of St Ann. She left Canada in 1876 to return to San Francisco to look after her elderly mother. As soon as her mother died, she took off again, this time south.

For more than twenty years in camps all over California and Arizona (including Tombstone, notorious for its connections to Wyatt Earp and his gang), Nellie ran hostels, funded other miners' claims, and led expeditions. When her brother-in-law died in 1881, Nellie moved her sister and five nieces and nephews west to live with her. When her sister died three years later, Nellie assumed responsibility for the young orphans.

She took them prospecting in Montana, Idaho, Wyoming, and New Mexico, nosing out new mines and making money out of buying and then selling mining claims. She even wrote articles for the newspaper about her claims – the extra publicity didn't do her any harm when it came time to sell. In her spare time she dabbled in politics and became known as a popular 'vote-catcher', campaigning successfully for the Republican governor of Arizona, Oakes Murphy. Nellie was generally travelling the country, but if she had a regular base it was in Tombstone. The people there still remember their Angel, even naming her birthday in August Nellie Cashman Day.

In 1897, Nellie heard about a stampede for gold to the Klondike, Yukon

Nellie Cashman's house, Tombstone, Arizona, photographed in 1937.

In the Klondike gold rush, Nellie crossed on foot from Alaska, USA, to British Columbia, Canada, via the harrowing Chilcoot Pass. She was in her mid-fifties at the time.

Territory in northern Canada – the Klondike Gold Rush. Aged fifty-two, she provisioned and prepared to head north once again, advertising in the papers that she would 'like to hear from anyone willing to fund the expedition with $5000 and six good miners' (*Tombstone Prospector*, 1897). She had a tumultuous time in Klondike, vying for business with other prospectors and miners, but she made a fortune. By 1904 she was able to sell her claim for $100,000.

Fairbanks, Alaska, was next. As well as mining here, she also set about raising money for a new hospital, St Matthews. It was said that she raised the cash by winning at cards.

In 1907, Nellie rounded up her dog pack and sled and headed north one more time – to a place called Nolan Creek. The seam here was rich but frozen solid until Nellie came up with the idea of using boilers and pipework to access the gold. Her system was used by miners for over a decade until new technology came in.

By 1920, Nellie was easing up on her mining work – but not on her travels. By now the septuagenarian was so famous that newspapers ran stories on her – one relates how, in one of her final journeys, this 'champion woman musher of the world' dog-sledded a distance of 750 miles through Alaska.

In the summer of 1924, Nellie realised she was weakening. She made her way to St Ann's Hospital in Victoria, which she had helped build decades before. She died there in January the following year, faithfully attended by nuns. She has been inducted into The Alaska Mining Hall of Fame and in 1984 she was also inducted into the Arizona Women's Hall of Fame. The US Postal Service has honoured her with a stamp.

AMY CARMICHAEL
1867–1951

Missionary in India who opened one of the country's
first orphanages

'There is no more tragic sight than the average missionary!'
Amy Carmichael, *God's Missionary* (1932)

orn in Millisle, Co Down, the eldest of seven siblings, Amy
Carmichael was from a middle-class, very religious Presbyterian background. When Amy was a teenager her parents moved to Belfast and
founded their own church, the Welcome Evangelical Church. She became
a Sunday School teacher there soon after.

The mission of evangelicals, such as Amy and her family, was to attract
the workers to their cause. These were people, many of them young women,
who had little in their world. They worked in sweated labour conditions,
that is, they got very little money for very long days, and no job security or
benefits of any kind. These young women of Belfast were known as Shawlies because, at a time when covering your head was deemed respectable
in public, they could not afford hats and had to use their shawls. For the
Shawlies, gathering with their friends to sing hymns and have the Bible
read to them as they relaxed must have seemed like heaven – and, from the
point of view of mill-owners, such as Amy's father, it had the advantage of
keeping them occupied and out of labour activism.

Amy Carmichael

Amy's work among the linen-mill workers made the mission a huge success. In 1887 her fundraising led to the building of Belfast's first Welcome Hall, which still stands today on Cambrai Street, Belfast, and which has a building named in her honour.

It seemed inevitable that Amy would one day want to branch out into missionary work abroad. First she went to Manchester, where the appalling conditions endured by the mill-workers proved a fertile hunting ground for conversions. While she was there, she was inspired by a lecture given by the China Inland Mission, an evangelical society, and decided to become a missionary herself.

The life of a missionary was often short and very hard. Many missionaries to African countries and the Indian subcontinent died within ten years, mainly of mosquito-borne diseases, such as malaria, which is still one of the world's biggest killers. Amy experienced several false starts. At one point, she was ready to sail for China but became ill with the painful neurological condition of neuralgia and could not travel. After her recovery, she sailed to Japan, but became so ill there with the same condition that she had to return home. Amy eventually took off again and this time she settled in Southern India, first in Bangalore and then further south in Tamil Nadu.

Amy made it her business to work with young, poor girls. The local custom was that, if there were an unwanted female child in a family due to poverty or the prioritising of boys, such girls might be left at a Hindu temple. Here they were consecrated as workers to the gods, and the best that could happen to them was domestic slavery, the worst, prostitution. Inspired by just one girl she had met who had run away from a temple, Amy's mission was to save as many of the girls as she could from such a life.

Missionary Amy Carmichael, wearing local dress and speaking to two children at the Dohnavur Fellowship, early 1900s.

In 1901 she founded the Dohnavur Fellowship in the province of Tamil Nadu as a safe haven for escaping temple women and girls. Here they were fed and looked after, their health was examined and any children born to them were cared for. Although they were still allowed to retain South Indian names and dress, they were encouraged, not to say pressured, to reject Hinduism and embrace Christianity. At one point, there were several hundred women and girls in the mission, and they all called Amy 'Amma', or Mother.

In 1912 she added a hospital to the Dohnavur Mission. By now, she had taken after her evangelical parents and formed her own lay religious order, named Sisters of the Common Life, comprising both Indian and European women who lived among the girls. Their motto was 'Love to live, live to love'.

Amy continued actively in her orphanage work until she suffered a bad fall when she was in her early sixties, which severely limited her mobility. Still full of religious zeal, she took to writing with a vengeance, publishing at least thirty religious books, including *The Gold Cord* (1932), the story of Dohnavur. She died in India aged eighty-three, and although temple prostitution has been long-outlawed, the Dohnavur Fellowship, now run by Indian Christians, continues to support local women and girls.

ANNIE MOORE
1874–1924

First person to enter America through Ellis Island
Immigration Office

'Give me your tired, your poor,
Your huddled masses yearning to breathe free,
The wretched refuse of your teeming shore.
Send these, the homeless, tempest-tossed, to me:
I lift my lamp beside the golden door.'
Inscription on the Statue of Liberty, from 'The New
Colossus' (1883), Emma Lazarus

Annie (christened Anna) Moore was born into extreme poverty in Cork city. In 1888 Annie's parents made the hard decision that hundreds of thousands had made before them – they left Ireland for America. They took their eldest son, but the rest of their children, Annie and her two younger brothers remained with relatives. The Moores were lucky – it took only two years before the passage money could be saved and sent to Annie and her brothers.

The siblings set sail from Cobh (then Queenstown) in the hard winter of 1891 on the SS *Nevada* bound for New York, and when they arrived on New Year's Day 1892, they claimed it was Annie's fifteenth birthday

A packed steamship on its way to Ellis Island.

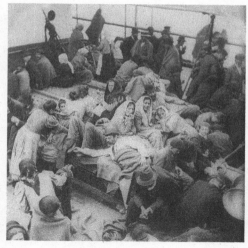

(she was actually seventeen). The gangplank was lowered, the children were pushed forward and found that they were to have the honour of being the first people processed through the new Ellis Island Immigration Office.

The idea behind Ellis Island was that newcomers should undergo medical and immigration checks – the medical to spot any obvious diseases, and the immigration to ensure those entering the country were planning on looking for work and were not criminals. If there was a problem, the immigrants could be kept on Ellis Island until this was resolved. Only steerage or third-class passengers such as Annie had to disembark and get in line to be processed through Ellis Island; the first and second classes were interviewed aboard ship in the comfort of their own cabins.

In contrast with the more than 12 million 'huddled masses' that came through Ellis Island after her, Annie, received VIP treatment that January morning. According to *The New York Times* there was an elaborate welcoming/opening ceremony for the 'little rosy-cheeked Irish girl' and she received a $10 gold piece! She must have gazed at the Statue of Liberty and thought she'd gone to heaven.

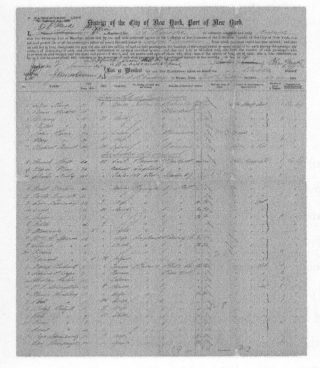

The manifest, or list of passengers, on the SS Nevada.

When all the 700 immigrants had been processed, they were required to buy their tickets for onward transports. This was either a ferry for New York, or a shuttle to various train stations across the United States. Incidentally the first person to buy an onward train ticket at Ellis Island was another Irish girl, the enterprising Ellie King from Waterford, who was on her way to Nebraska.

As for Annie and her brothers, they joined the rest of the family in Monroe St, Manhattan, where they lived in one of the new tenement blocks. She led a law-abiding life on the Lower East Side, married a bakery clerk and had eleven children. Annie's was a hard life; work was unremitting and at least four of her children died as infants.

Annie died of heart failure, aged only fifty. Her previously unmarked grave in Calvary Cemetery, Queens, has now been decorated with a handsome Celtic cross. There are also two statues of Annie sculpted by Jeanne Rhynhart – one at her port of departure in Cobh, Co Cork, and one at the Ellis Island facility, which closed down in 1952, and is now a museum.

This bronze statue of Annie Moore and her brothers in Cobh, Co Cork, has a counterpart in Ellis Island.

CARMEL SNOW
1887–1961

Legendary editor of *Harper's Bazaar* magazine

'Elegance is good taste plus a dash of daring.'
Carmel Snow

The work ethic and self-belief of Carmel Snow made her the template for many a tough fashion editor on both sides of the Atlantic.

Carmel White was born into a middle-class family in Dalkey, south Co Dublin. When Carmel was six, her father, a wool manufacturer, died unexpectedly. Her mother had to step forward and represent both him and the country in the Irish Pavilion in the Chicago World's Fair of 1893. This extraordinary woman, whose determination Carmel said she had inherited, then stayed on in Chicago to start a successful Irish goods emporium. She sent for her children one by one, as she could afford it.

After being farmed out to relatives while her mother was away, and a somewhat sketchy education, Carmel was 'finished' for a year in Belgium, as befitted an upper-class girl. She regularly attended Paris fashion shows and this started her off in fashion. Her mother, meanwhile, had bought a successful dressmakers in Manhattan. Carmel joined her mother and worked for her, developing her famous 'eye' for style. Her course was set.

Carmel trained at the dressmakers until in 1921, aged thirty-four, she landed a plum job at American *Vogue* on the editorial staff. Here she

The beautifully-dressed Carmel Snow as a young fashion editor, c.1930s.

attended shows, spotted trends and wrote features, and became the protégée of publisher Condé Nast. She soon was regarded as a fashion oracle.

In 1926 at the advanced age of nearly forty, this inveterate professional surprised everybody by marrying. The groom was a prominent society lawyer, Palen Snow, and the couple had four children. Carmel's only son was so premature he could not survive long in the days before neo-natal intensive care units. For the first and only time in her career, Carmel took time off. She stayed home with her baby and nursed him until he died in her arms aged just four weeks.

In 1932 she made the decision to move jobs from *Vogue* to its rival magazine *Harper's Bazaar*, owned by William Randolph Hearst. It was the right decision but Condé Nast never forgave her. She became editor-in-chief in 1934, and it was here, over the next twenty-four years that she became a New York legend.

She made *Harper's Bazaar* more than a fashion magazine. It was packed with pieces about fiction, events, arts and culture, as well as fashion. In 1940s America, Carmel Snow could make or break a career. She was the discoverer and mentor of new creative talents, such as Andy Warhol, Diana Vreeland, Henri Cartier-Bresson, Maeve Brennan, Lauren Bacall, Cecil Beaton, Christian Dior, Richard Avedon, Cristóbal Balenciaga … the list goes on. Three of her most successful protégés were Dior (for whom she coined the term 'New Look' to describe his clothes), Balenciaga (whose hats and suits she wore), and Diana Vreeland (who eventually eclipsed her).

In this period, Carmel was also credited with creating the first-ever outside fashion shoot, when she took a photographer and a model to a windy beach, and asked them to run around and produce spontaneous, free images, instead of the static tableaux the public were used to.

'I ran a three-ring circus with my family, my work and my social life,' she said, a sentiment any working parent can relate to – even one without the pearls and lavender-coloured hair of a fashion icon. Of course, being rich and having staff at work and at home must have been a help.

After the war, Carmel was the first fashion journalist who went back to France. In 1949 she received the Légion d'honneur from the French government for 'her influence in re-establishing French design in the United States'.

In 1953 Carmel came back to Ireland, followed by an entourage of fashion buyers. She had talent-spotted Irish designer Sybil Connolly and had decided to throw her considerable influence behind Irish collections featuring tweed, lace and linen at a show in Dunsany Castle. It was a make-or-break moment for Irish fashion when Carmel Snow swept in and changed the fashion landscape forever. Within six months Sybil was on the cover of *Life* magazine; six months after that she was the designer of choice for movie stars.

However, Carmel finally did a thing that women – especially fashion women – are never supposed to: she grew old and irrelevant. In 1957, the seventy-year-old doyenne was forced out of *Harper's*.

Carmel had always remained loyal to Ireland, holidaying there in the summer, and she tried to fulfil a dream of retirement by moving to the beautiful west of Ireland. But the toast of New York found it too bleak and lonely. She moved back to New York within the year, where she died in her sleep, aged seventy-three.

DID YOU KNOW?

* * *

After the 1798 Rising, **Mary Dwyer** née Doyle (*c.*1780–1861) from the Glen of Imaal in Wicklow, went on the run with her husband, United Irishman Michael Dwyer. They hid out for five years in the Wicklow Mountains. She is said to have taken part in guerrilla warfare and tricked a local landlord into a fatal ambush. When Michael was transported to New South Wales, Australia, after the 1803 Rising, she followed. Mary was buried twice in Australia – once in 1861 when she died, and then again in 1898, as Irish Australians commemorated the 1798 Rising.

* * *

Jane Mitchel née Verner (*c.*1821–1899) from Verner's Bridge, Armagh, became as ardent a republican as her husband, the Young Irelander John Mitchel. She followed John from Newry to Tasmania, and from Paris to the American South, experiencing war, shipwreck, and the death of five of her children on the way. Yet despite her radical political views about Ireland, she, like John, was a supporter of slavery and the slave trade.

* * *

A teenaged girl named **Kate Shelley** (1865–1912) from Offaly saved the lives of 200 people in her adopted home of Iowa. One stormy night in 1881, when Kate was just seventeen, a bridge over the Des Moines River collapsed. Realising that a trainload of passengers was hurtling towards it, Kate crawled over the only surviving bridge above a torrent and in the dark to raise the alarm. Her courage earned her a scholarship to college.

Johanna 'Annie' Sullivan (1866–1936), whose parents fled Limerick for Massachussetts during the Great Famine, became a pioneering educator for the deaf/blind despite being near-blind herself. She is the subject of a film, *The Miracle Worker*. Her only pupil and lifelong friend Helen Keller knocked out two of Annie's teeth when she started working with her.

Helen Keller with her lifelong teacher and friend, Annie Sullivan (standing).

* * *

THE WRONG SIDE OF THE LAW

*'I would rather get drunk on whiskey
than on champagne.'*
May Churchill Sharpe

DARKEY KELLY

*d.*1761

Ireland's first known serial killer

'The female of the species is more deadly than the male.'
Rudyard Kipling

Witch-burning, a titled rake, infanticide, the diabolical Hell-fire Club – the Dublin legend of Darkey Kelly has got the lot.

The local legend goes that, in the mid-1700s, a woman called Dorcas 'Darkey' Kelly ran a brothel called the Maiden Tower in Copper Alley, opposite Christ Church Cathedral in Dublin, on the very spot where the Darkey Kelly pub now stands. Among Darkey's variable clientele was Simon Luttrell, later the Earl of Carhampton – and also incidentally a member of Dublin's infamous Hellfire Club. The Hellfire Club was a group of wealthy sociopaths, who met in the Wicklow Mountains for a wide variety of nefarious activities, including abduction and torture of waifs and strays.

The legend says that when Darkey got pregnant with Simon's child and demanded money from him, the Hellfire side of his character surfaced. He took their baby and killed it in a satanic ritual known as a Black Mass, and then blamed the infant's death on Darkey. Darkey was found guilty of witchcraft and sentenced to a woman's death – tied to a stake,

Ghost stories, including one about Darkey Kelly, abound in Dublin.

half-strangled until unconsciousness and burnt. But that's not the whole story, which is somewhat more complicated.

It seems the name of Darkey Kelly, the brothel-keeper who died at the stake in 1761, has become confused with another brothel madam, Maria Llewellyn, who got on the wrong side of the Luttrells some time later. Maria was described as the 'foster-sister' of Simon Luttrell's son Henry. This is a connection that is less unlikely than it sounds. In the eighteenth century an aristocrat's son would have had a wet nurse to feed him and Henry's nurse (who had just given birth to her own daughter) was referred to by Henry as his foster mother. Therefore her daughter, Maria, might have seen herself as his foster sister.

In any case, Henry Luttrell was an even worse character than his father. Records show that he was a patron of Maria's establishment until the night when he raped a twelve-year-old girl there. Again, far from bringing a peer to trial, it was easier for the law to blame the madam, who was charged as an accessory to the rape, found guilty and sentenced to hang in 1788. However, Maria had powerful supporters, including the Lord Lieutenant of Ireland, and he commuted her sentence to the payment of a fine. The later confusion about identity arose because it was reported in error that Madam Darkey was Madam Maria's sister and so the two stories became linked.

And as for the real documented Darkey Kelly? She was indeed a brothel madam, but she had nothing to do with the Luttrells. Instead, her story is even more gruesome. When she was accused of killing one of her clients, shoemaker John Dowling, she was arrested and a search of her premises uncovered the decomposing bodies of no fewer than five men hidden in the cellars. Darkey was found guilty of murder, not witchcraft, and sentenced to be burnt alive near St Stephen's Green in 1761. Her horrific death caused rioting by a large mob of prostitutes, who took her body and buried it in an unknown location. Darkey is said to be Ireland's first serial killer.

In the mid-1700s capital punishments for crimes ranging from murder and treason to wounding, theft and arson were on an upward trend. The difference was that women were much more likely to go to the stake than the gallows. For example, if a woman murdered her husband or employer, or if she counterfeited money, she would most likely be burned, whereas men committing the same crimes would be hanged. The differing treatments of men and women regarding capital punishment eventually came to be seen for what it was — a savage and misogynistic medieval throwback, and by 1790 the burning of women was abolished in Ireland.

The traditional Irish music pub Darkey Kelly, opposite Christ Church, is said to be built on the site of Dorcas Kelly's brothel, and her ghost is said to walk the area around St Audeon's, close by Christ Church Cathedral.

CATHERINE FLANAGAN

(1829–1884)

AND MARGARET

HIGGINS

(1843–1884)

The Black Widows of Liverpool

'She'll never have to comb a grey hair.'
Catherine Flanagan about one of her victims

In crime fiction, poisoning has the reputation of being the favoured method of female killers. In the nineteenth century, poisons, such as arsenic and strychnine, and what would today be called Class A drugs, such as opium, were freely available over the counter of any chemist, as pesticides and medicines. The link with women seems also to have appeared because poisoning was not overtly violent, it was stealthy, and it could easily take place behind closed doors in the domestic space – the woman's domain.

The case of Irish sisters, Catherine and Margaret, took the female

After the Great Famine, the Irish packed into slums in Liverpool, Manchester and London. These were often known as rookeries.

poisoner cliché to new heights.

They were from a large, poor family in an unknown part of Ireland and fourteen years apart in age. Who knows what privations they suffered as children, but when they emigrated to Liverpool, like so many Irish of the time, Catherine was a young adult and Margaret a little girl, and they lived near the docks, in the heart of the Skirving Street slum.

Money was so tight it was not unusual for several families to share a small flat. By 1880 Catherine was a widow living with two Irish families, consisting of a father and daughter each, plus her own twenty-two-year-old son John and his wife, Mary. As well as subletting this flat, she was also known to lend money locally at high interest. What wasn't known at the time was that she had another means of making money. She was paying life insurance on named people, so that in the event of their death, she would receive a payout. And the names on the policy? Her son and daughter-in-law, John and Mary. In 1880, only a few months apart, the young couple died of dysentery, and Catherine, the grieving mother, collected insurance of more than £5000 in today's money.

Catherine's sister Margaret came to live in the house and in 1882, she married one of Catherine's lodgers, Thomas Higgins, while Catherine got into a relationship with the other lodger, Patrick Jennings. By the autumn of 1882 Thomas's eight-year-old daughter was showing symptoms of dysentry, and by November that year she was dead. Margaret received a large insurance payout for her stepdaughter.

Astonishingly, right up until this case, there was nothing to prevent anyone taking out insurance against someone else's life *without their knowledge*. You simply opened a policy in their name, paid a few shillings a week into it and, if they died, collected the money that was meant for their funeral expenses.

Just a few months after little Mary Higgins' death, Patrick Jennings' daughter, Margaret Jennings, also took ill and died of apparently the same illness. Another payout was collected, this time by Catherine. Patrick Jennings left the family home, and in so doing probably saved his own life.

By now, gossip was beginning to swirl around the sisters' household. The sisters and the grieving Thomas moved to a new flat, but within months Thomas was showing the same symptoms as his daughter – loss of appetite and crippling stomach pains. He died in October 1883.

His brother, Pat Higgins, horrified that his healthy hod-carrying brother had died so suddenly, brought the case to the attention of the police. While the body of Thomas was still at home being waked by the sisters and the neighbours, the coroner and his assistants burst into the house and demanded a full autopsy be carried out. Catherine knew the game was up – and she let herself out of the back door and went on the run, leaving her sister to be arrested on suspicion of murdering Thomas Higgins. She didn't get far; she was caught within the week and imprisoned alongside her sister.

Of course, the autopsy showed signs of arsenic poisoning. Not only on Thomas, but the exhumations and autopsies of three of the young people who had died, John, Mary and Margaret, also showed arsenic. The sisters had been soaking flypapers, which were coated in arsenic, in water and giving the water to their victims. And the motive? The insurance money.

They blamed each other for the killings and Catherine incriminated a group of four or five women in the insurance fraud part of the crime. But in the end, there was not enough evidence to convict the fraud ring, and only Catherine and Margaret were convicted of Thomas Higgins' murder. They were hanged on 3 March 1884 at Kirkdale Jail, now HMP Liverpool. Afterwards, it was felt that they had been responsible for at least five other deaths, possibly including Catherine's first husband, John Flanagan.

ELLEN KELLY
c.1832–1923

The mother of two members of the infamous Kelly gang,
Australian bushrangers

*'The trooper pulled out his revolver and said he would blow her
brains out if she interfered in the arrest [but Mother] told him it
was a good job for him Ned was not there or he would ram the
revolver down his throat ...'*

Jerilderie letter, dictated by Ellen's son, Ned (1880)

Around 1841, James and Mary Quinn sailed with their daughter Ellen, aged about nine, and at least six of her siblings on a government-sponsored ship from Belfast. 'Government-sponsored' is one way of saying that they were forced out of their country by the authorities. Fenianism was dangerously on the rise in the north and the government in London were getting as many disaffected Catholics as possible as far away as they could. Thus the Quinns were 'assisted migrants' rather than willing emigrants. Their hatred of British colonial authority was to be a feature of their lives when they got to Australia.

Ellen's family landed at Port Phillip, Victoria, southeast Australia in the earliest years of its existence. The Quinns lived in a tent for several years, then pushed on inland to a better life. The father worked as a porter, and

Ellen Kelly as an elderly woman with two of her grandchildren.

through hard work eventually saved enough money to buy some cows and rent a smallholding in Wallan, 45 km (28 miles) north of Melbourne.

One day Ellen's father took a man home from the pub. That man was John 'Red' Kelly, a recently released convict from Tipperary, sent to Van Diemen's Land (Tasmania) in 1841, some say for stealing pigs and some say for shooting a landlord. Red had served his sentence and was now emancipated.

Nowadays Australia prides itself on social and class mobility, and being connected with an early convict is not a stigma but a badge of honour. But in early Australia, there was massive snobbery. There was snobbery on the part of the colonial élite for what they called the 'bog Irish' arriving in numbers in Victoria, but there was even worse snobbery on the part of these same Irish, or 'free settlers', for those of their countrymen that were ex-convicts.

So when Ellen fell for Red (who had concealed his convict past) her father strongly opposed the marriage. But the future mother of outlaws recognised no paternal authority over her, and in 1850, pregnant by Red, she eloped with him to Melbourne. She was eighteen years old.

The newlyweds settled in Beveridge, about 48 km (30 miles) north of Melbourne. Life was hard for the Kellys and soon Red returned to a life of crime. Ellen had baby after baby; her eldest son, the infamous Ned, was born in 1855. In 1867, Red was released from a longish jail term for stealing cow hides but died the following year, leaving Ellen a homeless young widow with seven children.

In general, Irish settlers loathed local authority in the shape of the police – despite the fact that most of the police were first- or second-generation

Irish themselves. They looked on the police and judiciary in Melbourne as a mere extension of the landlords and lackeys of the government that had, as Ned later wrote in his famous Jerilderie letter, 'destroyed, massacred and murdered' the Irish people. Now the extended Quinn and Kelly families also held the authorities responsible for the death of Red.

After Red's death Ellen Kelly moved her family nearer to Quinn relations at Wangaratta, northeast Victoria. She farmed eighty-eight acres of untamed land at Eleven Mile Creek with the help of her brothers and sons. Of course the menfolk disrespected local law and order and did as they pleased with the land and the stock. They also did as they pleased with their own family; Ellen's brother-in-law got ten years in prison for burning down her home after a row. Several of her brothers were also convicted of crimes ranging from horse theft to arson. Ellen, too, was hauled into court several times for violent outbursts and, soon, her own boys, Ned and Dan, were in trouble.

The rampage of the Kelly gang, which has passed into folklore, lasted for just a few years in the late 1870s. Ned, Dan, Joe Byrne and Stephen Hart waged war on the local stock-owners of the King Valley region, by clever stunts and ever more daring escapades. They stole horses. They destroyed fences – a big problem in massive farms of several thousand acres. They drove cattle onto their land and rebranded it as their own. Aided and abetted by Ellen, they made and sold industrial amounts of illegal moonshine whiskey. The authorities in turn waged war on them and their family.

The Kelly boys lived at home when they weren't on the run, and visits by the local law were constantly made to the house of Ellen, who was always known as the 'notorious Mrs Kelly'. (She had in fact married again, a Californian named George King, who abandoned her and their three young children.)

In 1878 a Constable Fitzpatrick, with whom the boys had a long-running feud, paid a visit to the Kelly home. He found Ellen, her newborn baby and her teenage daughter at home. Ellen would later claim that the constable tried to sexually assault her daughter so she had been forced to hit him over the head with a spade. At that point Ned came home and shot the constable in the hand before running away. The constable survived his injury but Ellen was arrested and got three years with hard labour for her part in the Fitzpatrick affair. Voicing popular condemnation of Ned Kelly's mother, the *Ovens and Murray Advertiser* judged that 'crime is hereditary'.

After that incident the Kelly gang were now outlaws, literally 'outside the law's protection', which meant they could be shot and killed by anyone and there would be no consequences. They bushranged all over the territory and eventually turned to bank robbery. The job that was to spell the end for them was at Jerilderie, a town in New South Wales.

Ned and his gang robbed the bank. Police pursued them but could not find them; instead Ned and his gang found *their* camp and held it up. There was a gun battle at a place known as Stringybark Creek, and Ned killed three of the policemen. He was now wanted for murder.

He was on the run for two years before being taken in the famous Glenrowan siege, during which he famously wore a homemade suit of iron from top to toe. Despite this, he was shot several times in the arms and legs, and his brother Dan and the rest of the gang were burnt to death in a shack.

While waiting trial, Ned Kelly vented his spleen at the treatment of himself and his family in a famous document known as the Jerilderie letter:

I have been wronged, and my mother ... has no alternative only to put up
with the brutal and cowardly conduct of a parcel of big ugly fat-necked
wombat-headed big-bellied magpie-legged narrow-hipped splawfooted
sons of Irish bailiffs or English landlords, which is better known as
Officers of Justice or Victorian Police ...

Ned was hanged on 11 November 1880 at Melbourne Jail, while Ellen
sat in a nearby cell, listening. It is said that her last words to him were
'Mind you die like a Kelly, son.' One of his final wishes was that his mother
be released. The request was denied and she served her full time.

An unfair trial, a huge amount of local popular support, and a spectac-
ular funeral ensured that the eldest son of Ellen Kelly is remembered as a
daring, attractive folk hero, commemorated in film and song, instead of a
dangerous career criminal. His brother, Ellen's youngest son, went on to
join the hated police force and achieved fame as a rodeo rider.

Ellen Kelly lived to bury seven of her twelve children. She died aged
ninety-one in 1923, and is buried in an unmarked grave.

JOSEPHINE 'CHICAGO JOE' HENSLEY

1844–1899

Sex industry entrepreneur in the Wild West

'Notice is given by Mrs Josephine Hensley that parties who sell
her husband liquor or who allow him to gamble in
their premises will be prosecuted.'
Semi-Weekly Miner (December 1882)

The woman who became known as Chicago Joe was born Mary Welch (or Walsh). She was just a teenager when she arrived in New York from an unknown location in Ireland. Initially, young Mary would have worked any cleaning job she could find, but soon she fell on hard times and into prostitution. As a 'working girl', she changed her name to the more Anglo-Saxon-sounding Josephine Airey.

The mid-1860s were a tumultuous time for America. The Civil War had ended in 1865, and it was the heyday of the frontierspeople pushing ever westward. Gold rushes seemed to be everywhere and the United States was experiencing a boom beyond its wildest dreams. Josephine was an astute

In the days before the railway, the trail Chicago Joe took to Helena, Montana, was hard-going.

woman. She knew she could make it big but she needed to follow the money. She moved first to Chicago and then in 1867 she joined a trail and headed west to Helena, Montana.

The trail to Helena had only been 'blazed' (ie opened up by speculators) five years earlier, but already it was booming. Gold had been discovered. Where there are mines, there are miners. And where there are miners there are saloons and brothels. In Helena, there were nine men for every one woman, and prostitution – which was not actually illegal until 1885 – was a business with a lot of scope for expansion. There were so many paying customers and so few women that Josephine soon transformed herself from a working girl into a madam, presiding over the red light district of Helena like a queen. She bought her own saloon/dancehall, known as the Red Light Saloon, and started to recruit her employees from Chicago, giving rise to her nickname 'Chicago Joe'.

According to the *Anaconda Standard* of October 1875, Josephine spent the next decade raking in dollars. She paid the passages to America of many of her relatives in Ireland, establishing some in business and educating their children.

In 1875 Helena became the state capital of Montana. Chicago Joe was delighted – she could now charge more money from her new affluent clientele. At her height, the *Anaconda Standard* reckoned she possessed diamonds worth $20,000.

Lavish jewellery and beautiful clothes show how well Chicago Joe was doing in her 1880s heyday.

In 1878, aged thirty-four, Josephine married James Hensley and further added to her veneer of respectability. They gave lavishly to charities, and his gambling and drinking did not affect their prosperity – and popularity – as philanthropic, generous leaders of society in Helena. A steamer was even named after Josephine.

She bought another, even bigger brothel and various other properties around Helena, making her one of the town's biggest landlords, and giving her a voice in the town. The jewel in Josephine's crown was The Coliseum, a sumptuous, brand-new vaudeville theatre. 'Those with times on their hands can while away an hour very pleasantly,' trumpeted the *Helena Independent* of 1893 at its opening, certainly a euphemism, since one floor of The Coliseum was furnished as a brothel.

But it was too good to last. In the 1890s the town was moving away from its Wild West days where anything could happen, and legal challenges were surfacing about the exact nature of Josephine's now-illegal businesses. She fought off several court cases – but she could not fight off a nationwide recession.

The recession of 1893–1897 was an unromantic way for a formidable racketeer such as Josephine to meet her match – but it did for her nevertheless. Her properties were mortgaged and she lost them all, except for the Red Light Saloon. She and James moved into a room above the saloon, and eked out a poor living there.

These conditions contributed to her early death from pneumonia in 1899. In an echo of her glory days, her funeral was a lavish affair paid for by the town, and, once again, Chicago Joe made all the newspapers.

LIZZIE HALLIDAY
*c.*1859–1918

First woman to be condemned to the electric chair

'The worst woman on Earth!'
The New York Times (1918)

Sometimes known as 'The Gypsy Queen' and sometimes simply as 'The Worst Woman on Earth', Lizzie's 1894 trial for triple murder was a sensation that gripped America.

According to contemporary newspaper reports, Lizzie was born Eliza McNally in Co Antrim, and emigrated to America as an eight-year-old. In 1879, aged twenty, she was married for the first time, to a Charles Hopkins. She gave birth to a baby boy, whom she may have left in an orphanage. Charles died after two years, and Lizzie married again, a much older man named Brewer, described as a veteran from the American Civil War. He died within the year.

Lizzie then married a friend of Brewer's, named George Smith, another veteran, and allegedly tried to poison him with tea. After he discovered her design, she fled to Vermont, taking everything portable of value from the house. There she (bigamously) married Charles Playstel, but lived with him only two weeks before decamping to Philadelphia, to take refuge in the house of old neighbours from Antrim, the McQuillans.

From there Eliza returned to New York, and married yet another older man, Paul Halliday. It wasn't long before she strayed again. She eloped with one of the neighbours, stealing a team of horses to do so. At this point the law got involved, and Lizzie was charged with theft. Because of her chaotic past and lurid reports by her neighbours of her increasingly bizarre behaviour, the court declared her insane and sent her to an asylum to complete a short sentence.

On her release, Paul Halliday took her back. It proved to be a tragic mistake for, not long after her return, their home mysteriously burned down, with Paul's disabled son trapped inside. The boy died. Although Lizzie was widely thought to have started the fire, there was no hard evidence linking her with the crime.

A few months later, Lizzie told her neighbours that her husband Paul had gone on a trip. They were very suspicious. So suspicious that one day when Lizzie was out, her neighbours searched the property. But instead of finding the body of Paul as they had expected, they found two other bodies in an outhouse, both women. They had been shot.

The bodies in the barn were the remains of Mrs McQuillan and her daughter, the kind people from Antrim and Philadelphia, who had tried to help Lizzie. It seems that the McQuillans had been approached by Lizzie and enticed away – first mother and then daughter – with an offer of work. Lizzie was arrested, a more thorough search was made of the property, and it was then that the body of her husband was discovered under the floorboards of her house.

Her trial by jury took place in the summer of 1894. There was little question she had carried out the murders; her defence was insanity.

The electric chair, a new and 'humane' method of execution in 1890s America.

Her behaviour in prison was disturbed in the extreme. In three separate attempts at suicide, she went on hunger strike, attempted to hang herself and slashed her own throat with a piece of glass. She was such a danger to herself and others that she was eventually chained to the floor. Her plea for insanity certainly seemed to have some grounds.

The latest scientific tests were carried out by a Dr EC Mann, acting for the prosecution. They included examining the state of her skin, which was found to be moist from perspiration. But perspiring, according to the experts in mental illness of the time, was something that a genuine lunatic could never do, no matter what stress they were under. Another piece of cast-iron, fool-proof evidence presented by Dr Mann claimed that an insane person would never try to hide a crime – which Lizzie evidently had. On the basis of these tests, the plea of insanity was thrown out and Lizzie was found guilty of first degree murder. She had not testified on her own behalf.

She was sentenced to 'death by electricity'– the first woman ever to receive this pronouncement. By reason of clemency, her sentence was commuted by Governor Flowers of New York: 'I do not think her a fit subject for the death penalty. It will be much safer to commute the sentence to life imprisonment.'

The Governor had meant safer in a legal sense, rather than the literal sense, but the sad story of Lizzie was not over yet. More than ten years after her committal to the asylum, and long before safety protocols were put in place to safeguard both patients and their carers, 'the worst woman on Earth' got into a room alone with a young nurse, Nellie Wicks, and stabbed the nurse more than 200 times with her own scissors. The murder of Nellie led to a change in safety rules for asylums across America. But it was too late for Lizzie; she spent the rest of her life in solitary confinement.

'TYPHOID MARY' MALLON
1869–1938

The first asymptomatic carrier of typhoid

'She came out fighting and swearing, both of which she could do with appalling efficiency and vigor.'
Fighting for Life, Dr S Josephine Baker (1939)

The strange story of 'Typhoid Mary' Mallon is an early example of how press coverage in early twentieth-century America could ruin a life. Even today the nickname of Typhoid Mary is jokingly used to refer to any sneezers, sniffers and coughers.

Mary emigrated from Co Tyrone to New York in 1884 when she was fifteen. Like many young Irish women before her, she found work as a domestic servant and, over the next ten years, worked her way up to becoming a cook. There was plenty of work and Mary did not need to stay in one place long. She was able to hire out her services at will and make enough money to live on and to send home to Ireland.

In 1906, while Mary was employed in the holiday home of the wealthy Warren family in Long Island, there was a sudden unexplained outbreak of typhoid, a potentially fatal bacterial infection. Three children and their mother fell seriously ill.

As health inspectors investigated, they found that this was not the first time it had happened. In six years, no fewer than seven families that Mary had worked for in New York City had experienced typhoid with some forty people falling ill. One woman had died.

It was enough for the authorities to want to take her in.

But Mary was not compliant. When an investigator named George Soper was called in, he found it difficult to track her down. And when he did find her, she physically fought with officers and tried to run.

She claimed she had never been ill – but, in fact, she had probably had a mild form of the disease and ignored it. Stool and blood tests were taken and these proved that Mary was carrying the typhoid bacillus. She had become America's first healthy carrier of typhoid.

The authorities moved swiftly and decisively. They quarantined Mary in New York's North Brother Island where she lived in isolation for three years, her only company a dog. As time went by there were complaints about this unfair treatment of the woman, though she was still mocked in the popular press. 'A perambulating disease,' the *New York Tribune* called her in 1909, while the *Belding Banner* gleefully reported how 'a brave Michigan farmer has offered to wed Mary Mallon, the walking typhoid fever germ ... and take her to a secluded place ...'

Mary contacted a lawyer and in 1909 she was released – on condition that she never work with food again. She tried to keep her side of the conditions. She worked as a laundress, a much more arduous and less well-paid job than cooking. But after five years she reneged on the deal she had made with the health authorities. She changed her name to Mary Brown and

Mary Mallon infected more than fifty people while working as a cook.

TYPHOID
CARRIER →

← ANY FOOD
NOT COOKED
AFTER PREP-
ARATION

IN THIS MANNER THE FAMOUS "TYPHOID MARY" INFECTED FAMILY AFTER FAMILY

went back to work as a cook in a New York women's hospital.

In the typhoid outbreak that followed, two people died. Again, the authorities tracked down Mary and this time they made public her involvement and she became a national hate figure. Cartoons of her were all over the papers, of her stirring food as skulls fell into it. She was hounded out of work and accommodation. Eventually she was taken back into custody 'for her own safety'.

Mary Mallon spent the next twenty-three years back in the clinic on North Brother Island. She was in isolation for much of that time, but towards the end of her life she was allowed to work – as a bottle-washer in the kitchen. When she died after a stroke in 1938 a post mortem showed there was indeed live typhoid in her gall bladder.

MAY CHURCHILL SHARPE
1871/1876–1929

Career criminal

'I would rather get drunk on whiskey than on champagne.'
May Churchill Sharpe, *Chicago May: Her Story* (1928)

ay Churchill Sharpe aka May Duignan, May Avery, Diamond May, and many other aliases, was dubbed the 'Queen of Crooks' in contemporary newspapers. She was one of the first people to use the new-fangled science of photography for blackmail purposes (*The Irish Times*, 19 August 1999).

According to her autobiography *Chicago May: Her Story by May Churchill Sharpe*, published in 1928, she was a bad egg right from the start. She claims she was born Beatrice Desmond in 1876, though other sources have her name as Mary and her year of birth as 1871. She was one of seven children, six of whom were boys, in a prosperous farming family near Granard, Co Longford. She was often in trouble with the nuns at school and was sent home in disgrace several times.

May claims she was resentful of her parents' attempts to curb her behaviour and, aged thirteen, she stole the money from her father to leave home.

'Nothing easier than to rob the money box in father's room… he could afford to lose it, and I needed it… In the spring of 1889 I flew the coop with £60 and my clothes… I was heading for Londonderry.'

She went that way so she wouldn't be pursued by family. At first everything went well, with people along the way giving her shelter and feeding her, but 'past Enniskillen, I had to pay my way; and blarney was not money of the realm'. May soon took passage for America.

Once in Chicago, May immediately fell in with a crook named Dal Churchill and married him. He was lynched the following year after a robbery, leaving her a teenaged widow. At no point in her autobiography does May admit that, as well as being a pickpocket and petty criminal, she was also a prostitute, but it is impossible to believe that a young girl of her age avoided it as a way of making a living. What is sure is that she was proud of her status as 'a prize graduate in the Chicago school of crime' and continued without remorse: 'I have had no regrets', she wrote, 'except when caught'.

May was a globetrotter: New York, Rio de Janeiro, Paris, London, New York – anywhere she could get someone else to pay the bills and pick up some 'soft stuff' (money). Her take on the South American 'white-slave', or prostitution racket, is especially chilling: she notes that the girls in the brothels in Argentina and Brazil are between thirteen and eighteen years old because 'when a girl becomes eighteen she is soon passée. The Argentineans certainly like them young!'

May spent a third of her life in prison, mostly because of a big-time gangster called Eddie Guerin. After doing time for her part in his foiled

May Churchill Sharpe, sporting pearls and fashionably waved hair, 1920s.

robbery on the American Express office in Paris in 1901, she ran into him again in London in 1907. There was no love lost between the two; rows broke out and soon escalated. One night May was arrested for shooting and wounding him. This time she was sentenced to fifteen years for attempted murder.

She spent her sentence in Aylesbury Prison where, according to *The Irish Times*, she met Constance Markievicz. It is hard to believe that Constance would have been pleased at the prospect of meeting her countrywoman – after all, Constance repeatedly endured hunger strikes for the right to be treated as a political prisoner, which included not having to associate with common criminals, such as Chicago May.

On her early release in 1917, May travelled back to America, where her life slowly and inexorably fell apart. She again resorted to criminality, including robbery, assault, prostitution, attempted murder and, of course, blackmail. She took to drink and drugs, and was in and out of prison in New York, Detroit and Philadelphia. She refused to believe that prison ever helped her, and surprisingly, in her autobiography, came up with a political solution to the problem of crime. Devising a way to give everybody a decent job was essential, she maintained, public ownership of utilities would be a good start, and if that made her 'a Socialist', she didn't care!

The Washington Times of July 1922 named May the 'Queen of the Underworld' and when the New York papers ran a series of features on her life, she became famous. This seemed to have been a turning point for her, though she was clear about why: 'I only want to reform now from a business point of view' she wrote, that is, mining her life for stories was an easy way of making money.

Somewhat gallantly, she dedicated the volume to August Vollmer, Chief of Police, Berkeley CA, who she credited with first showing her 'a practical way to go straight'.

She did not get to enjoy her fame for long. May died the year after her book came out, at the early age of fifty-eight. She is buried in Philadelphia.

DID YOU KNOW?

In 1926, a middle-aged Dublin woman named **Violet Gibson** (1876–1956) shot Mussolini in an attempted assassination, wounding him in the nose. She was the sister of Lord Ashbourne, former President of the Gaelic League in London who, when he heard what she had done said, 'Poor dear.' It is thought that her attempt was counter-productive; it caused a wave of popular sympathy for Mussolini and strengthened the Fascist grip on Italy.

The case of convicted murderer **Grace Marks** (*c.*1828–*c.* after 1873) from Ulster was controversial in its time. She was present during the murders of her Canadian employer and his housekeeper, and was incarcerated for thirty years despite being only sixteen years old, and not proven to have play an active role. There is a novel based on Grace's life, *Alias Grace*, by the award-winning author Margaret Atwood.

Mary Daly (1865–1903) of Co Laois was hanged in Tullamore Jail for the murder of her husband on the evidence of her own children. She was the last woman hanged in Ireland under British rule.

According to the *Irish Times* of 7 September 2016, the last woman to receive capital punishment in Ireland was thirty-one-year-old **Annie Walshe** from Co Limerick, who was hanged for the murder of her husband, Ned. Her accomplice, Ned's nephew, was hanged beside her at Mountjoy Jail on 5 August 1925.

POETRY
AND PROSE

'Coileach bán ar chearcaibh, nó file mná i imbaile.'

'A white cock among hens, or a woman poet in a village.'

Munster proverb about bad luck

LÍADAIN

7th century

Poet

'Curithir, once a poet, I loved.
My grief! The profit has not reached me.
He in his cell is shut with God,
And I within these walls.'
Líadain and Curithir, retold by Moireen Fox (1917)

Poetry flourished in ancient Ireland. As part of the strict Brehon code by which the people lived for millennia, there was a respected class of ancient poets, whose job was to compose and perform poems about past glories, and to preserve royal genealogies in memory. Líadain was one such – but she has left none of her own poetry. Instead, she is famous for a ninth-century poem written about her and her tragic love affair with another poet, Curithir.

Originally from Corkaguiney, Co Kerry, the historical Líadain seems to have been in the highly unusual position of being in an occupation usually reserved for men. The Brehon custom of the seventh century was that poets travelled from fort to fort with the royal court, and the poem tells us that that is how Líadain met Curithir:

Líadain of the Corco Dubne, a poetess, went visiting
into the country of Connaught. There Curithir, Otter's son,
of Connaught, himself a poet, made an ale-feast for her.
"Why should not we two unite, Líadain?" saith Curithir.
"A son of us two would be famous."
"Do not let us do so", saith she, "lest my round of visiting
be ruined for me. If you will come for me again at my home,
I will go with you."

From *Líadain and Curithir, an Irish love-story of the ninth century*,
translated by Kuno Meyer (1902)

The idea to wait may have been because it broke the all-important
Brehon code of hospitality that they should become lovers while guests
in a royal house. On the other hand, it may be that Líadain was ambitious
as a court poet, and did not want to break her professional commitments.

The poem tells us that Curithir agreed to her condition, but when he

The decorative title pages of Líadain and Curithir.

arrived at the fort of Líadain's family, he found she had taken the veil, that is, become a nun. It is not clear why, but some modern interpretations have claimed it might have been because Líadain wanted the status of a poet, not a wife. However, Curithir still loved her so he decided to become a monk and the two made their way to a monastery run by Cummin the Tall, to seek his advice. He judged they could remain and talk every day, but added a tortuous twist: when they talked, they were not allowed to see each other.

Eventually Líadain challenged this probation and asked Cummin if they could look upon each other for one night. He agreed to let them spend the whole night together, in conversation, on condition that they maintain their chastity. Of course, the two lovers could not hold out. They broke their vow of chastity and Cummin banished Curithir forever.

Curithir spent the rest of his life roaming the world in penance for his sins, while Líadain spent the rest of her life mourning her lost love.

> A short while I was
> In the company of Curithir,
> Sweet was my intimacy with him.
> The music of the forest
> Would sing to me when with Curithir,
> Together with the voice of the purple sea.

Eventually Líadain lay down on the flagstone where they spent their one night together and died.

This story, as all ancient stories, changes through the centuries depending on who is doing the copying. The original was probably a pagan story, to do with the responsibilities and prohibitions placed on lovers in a stratified Brehon society. But after the monks had got hold of it in the ninth century, they changed the old ways to the new, the royal court to a monastery, and made sure the main characters repented of their ways before dying in the faith, instead of going out in a blaze of unrepentant pagan glory.

LÆTITIA PILKINGTON

*c.*1712–1751

Poet and satirist

'If ever a woman wanted a champion, it is obviously
Laetitia Pilkington.'
Virginia Woolf, *The Common Reader* (1928)

Described disparagingly in Victorian biographies as an 'adventuress', Laetitia made quite a journey in the 1730s, from a curate's wife to a saucy memoirist and famous satirist.

She was born into the Van Lewen family in Dublin *c.*1712, and lived conventionally and comfortably at a time when Georgian Dublin was experiencing prosperity. She enjoyed a middle-class upbringing with access to books and music, but no formal education. She was married very young to Matthew Pilkington, a Church of Ireland curate, around 1725.

The great satirist and national treasure, Jonathan Swift, took the pretty young couple under his wing and, with his help, Matthew published his *Poems* in 1730. The amusing Laetitia grew close to the great man. He teased her and taught her about language, and she amused and beguiled him. They traded books and poems – and Laetitia started to write.

I was most incorrigibly devoted to versifying, and all my spouse's wholesome admonitions had no manner of effect on me; I believe this scribbling itch is an incurable disease ...

The Memoirs of Mrs Laetitia Pilkington, Written by Herself, London (1748)

The Pilkington marriage was not happy. Matthew was penniless and always searching for a job. He was jealous of his clever little wife's 'versifying' abilities and her excellent memory for stories, which so impressed Swift. One anecdote concerns the 'rabble of Cavan':

I remember some years ago, when the Cavan rabble were up in arms, my mother, sister, and I, went to pay a visit at Rathfarnham. On our return home, we were surrounded by a pack of these wretches, who ordered my father's coachman to pull off his hat to them, which he refusing, and they being all armed with short thick oak tree clubs, they swore we should not ride in a coach, and they walk; my mother, with surprising presence of mind, said "Gentlemen, you are very welcome to the coach, my daughter and I will walk, to oblige you with it," which, villains, ruffians, and murderers as they were, they would not permit, but only desired we might huzza for them, this ... we cheerfully did; and my mother said, "Gentlemen, perhaps you are dry," and gave them a crown, with which they were so well pleased, that they huzza'd for us, offering to guard us safe to town; but she alleging that would be too much trouble, they left us with a kind assurance, that they would drink our healths, and fight for us any time we stood in need of their protection.

Amusing company she may have been but in 1732, Matthew left her to go to London as the Lord Mayor's chaplain, and soon found another love. Laetitia followed him to try and save their marriage. She later claimed he spent considerable effort trying to set her up with other men to give him an excuse for a divorce:

> I could scarcely regard Mr Pilkington as a husband; but rather a man whose property I was, and who would gladly dispose of me to the best bidder. Shocking thought!

The miserable couple returned to Dublin. Matthew filed for divorce in 1737. Ungallantly he cited his wife's adultery. (Laetitia slyly claimed that her husband had indeed caught her with a man in her bedroom, but they had been *reading* together.) Then he departed for London, leaving Laetitia with three children and no means of support.

What was Laetitia to do? A mid-eighteenth-century husband, such as Matthew, owned everything in the marriage, including the clothes on his wife's back. He locked away Laetitia's books, he locked her out of the garden – he even locked the tea casket. She was totally unacceptable to society, almost less than human, now that she was divorced.

In addition, deserted woman were vulnerable, and considered fair game for all. Laetitia came to the attention of the notorious Hellfire Club, a loose group of aristocratic kidnappers, torturers and rapists, based in the Dublin area. One night she was visited at home by the Earl of Ross, a founder member of the club. Along with some friends he attempted to abduct her for the purposes of rape. They were foiled by Laetitia barricading herself into her room and screaming bloody murder until the landlady came and threw them out.

Not long after the Hellfire incident, some people arrived at Laetitia's house and started to move in, and Laetitia realised Matthew had sold it. She now had nowhere to live so she took her children to her father-in-law, who passed them on to their father. Matthew bullied the 'little bastards', as he called them, claiming they weren't his (eventually he cut them out of his will). Laetitia could do nothing to help them. One of the most heinous laws of the land in the 1700s prevented a woman from having custody of her own children; since she was considered the possession of her husband, so were the children. In any case, she had no means to support them. Laetitia headed for London.

In the West End, Laetitia took lodgings opposite a famous gentlemen's club known as White's, which was frequented by the titled and rakish. There, to scrape a living, she rented her pen out on a poem-by-poem basis. Her versifying saved her from starvation, as she churned out ballads, satires, jokes and love letters for rich men to pass off as their own.

If a gentleman of the club was disparaging of her, she made him the subject of a biting satire, published for all to see. But if a gentleman sent her money, wine or food, he received a praise poem. She had learned her lessons well from Dean Swift.

But over the next ten years Laetitia slid inexorably down the social scale. She lived off gifts from wealthy literary men. A guinea here and a guinea there offered some, but not enough, protection. The novelist Samuel Richardson was one of her patrons, fascinated with the well-bred Irish lady living in a London slum. Theatre impressario and Poet Laureate Colley

Laetitia Pilkington by Nathaniel Hone the Elder.

Cibber was another; he kindly passed her work around. Often her days were spent walking from one rich mansion to another across town, asking for a shilling or two for poetry.

Eventually in 1742, with an increasing number of ex-landladies clamouring for unpaid rent, Laetitia ended up in Marshalsea Debtor's Prison (later made famous in *Little Dorrit*, the 1857 novel by Charles Dickens). 'Poor Laetitia is become the football of fortune,' she wrote sadly. She was extricated from prison by Samuel Richardson.

Laetitia's stroke of genius was to mine her memory for anecdotes from her life. The result was her scandalous *Memoirs*. According to *A Concise Dictionary of Irish Biography* (1928), clearly still sniffy after 180 years, these scribblings were 'only valuable for their anecdotes of Swift'. The memoirs were indeed full of anecdotes; they are the first known biography of Swift and give fascinating insights into the domestic situation of a man who was a household name in his own lifetime. (He deserved this early kiss-and-tell, having abandoned Laetitia after her divorce, and calling her 'the most profligate whore in two kingdoms'. Laetitia wrote: 'This is but a retaliation. No person who did not deserve a stripe ever got one from me.')

Pleasingly for Laetitia, her *Memoirs* were not only a means to settle scores against Dean Swift and her ex-husband, but they were also a showcase for her own talents as a writer, and a way of making money.

Once he heard that the *Memoirs* were in manuscipt form, Laetitia's ex-husband threatened every publisher in London so that none would touch it. Laetitia returned to Dublin, and found that the booksellers there had no such scruples. In 1748, with a new patron Sir Robert King in tow, Laetitia was able to publish the first two volumes of the *Memoirs*. They were, she said, a warning to all the lady readers, because 'reputation once gone is never to be retriev'd'.

She made enough money out of them to live in Ireland, but she was not to enjoy the fruits of her labours long. She died in 1751. The last volume of her *Memoirs* was published in 1754 by her son, John Carteret Pilkington.

MÁIRE BHUÍ NÍ LAOGHAIRE
1774–*c.*1840

Poet in the oral tradition

'Coileach bán ar chearcaibh, nó file mná i imbaile.'
'A white cock among hens, or a woman poet in a village.'
Munster proverb about bad luck

T hough she was not formally educated, Máire Bhuí Ní Laoghaire became a renowned poet in the traditional oral form.

She was born into a large farming family in the Muskerry area of Co Cork at a time when Ireland was seething with unrest over the unfair policies governing agricultural land use and ownership. By the early 1800s local groups, such as the Whiteboys, opposed rack rents, the obligation to pay tithes to the established church, and the onerous hearth tax. These groups were secret but were regularly discovered and crushed by the authorities.

Married at eighteen years of age to Séamus de Búrca, and settled in Keimaneigh (in Irish *Céim an Fhia*), Co Cork, Máire Bhuí recorded the unrest of the people and the unhappy state of her country in aislings and ballads. She did much to maintain hope of liberation in the Gaelic Munster of her time.

The lonely Pass of Keimaneigh in the 1920s.

Her most famous song, *Cath Chéim an Fhiaidh*, or *The Battle of Kei-maneigh* describes a confrontation between the Cork Whiteboys and the local yeomanry unit in 1822 – which ended indecisively. Here is the second stanza in Irish followed by a translation:

Níor fhan fear, bean ná páiste i mbun áitribh ná tí acu

Ach na gártha goil a bhí acu's na míle olagón

Ag féachaint ar an ngarda go 'teacht láidir ina dtimpeall

Ag lámhach is ag líonadh 's ag scaoileadh 'na dtreo.

An liú gur leath i bhfad i gcian

'S é dúirt gach fear, nur mhaith leis triall

'Gluaisígh go mear, tá an cath dá riar

Agus téim is ina gcomhair'

Thánadar na sárfhir, I gcoim áthais le Clanna Gael

Is thiománadar na páinthigh le fánaidh ar seol.

There remained no man, woman or child near me,

Looking after home about them,

Who was not shrieking, weeping and lamenting,

Looking at the soldiers surrounding them, loading and shooting and

firing at them.

The cry went out far and wide, every man saying that he wished

to turn out,

'Move quickly! The battle is under way and let's go and join it!'

The fine men came to the great joy of the Gaels,

and they drove the slobs downwards and away.

In the 1840s, a new landlord apparently raised the rent on Máire Bhuí. Her family were generous but had little savings to rely on. When she and her husband were evicted from their home, they went to live with their son Mícheál. She died towards the end of the 1840s, despite the date given on her gravestone at Inchigeelagh, Co Cork:

Go dtuga Dia

suaimhneas síoraí do

Mháire Bhuí Ní Laoire

1774–1840

da fear céile

Séamas De Búrca

1771–1847

Cois abhann ghleanna an Chéama

in Uíbh Laoire sea bhímse

mar a dtéann an fia san oíche

chun síorchodladh sóil

ag machnamh seal liom féinig

ag déanamh mo smaointe

ag éisteacht i gcoilltibh

le binnghuth na n-eon

Ag Críost an mhuir

Ag Críost an t-Iasc

I líonta Dé

Go gcastar sinn

She was survived by her poems and songs, which were sung and recited by local people for decades before finally being written down mostly by two local men in the 1890s, while some verses were later recorded by the Irish Folklore Commission.

MÁIRE MacNEILL

1904–1987

Folklorist and writer

'It is I would have given my dower
To have seen him set forth,
Whistling careless and gay in the grey of the morn.
By gorse bush and fraughan and thorn.'
Winifred Letts, from 'Spring, the Travelling Man' (1911)

Máire MacNeill was born in Portmarnock, Co Dublin, into a cultured family. Her father, Eoin MacNeill, was a founding member of the Gaelic League and became Professor of Early Irish History at UCD when Máire was four. Frequent family trips were made to the Gaeltacht and Irish and English were spoken at home.

Máire was eleven in 1915 when her father became Commander-in-Chief of the Irish Volunteers. When he was arrested after the Easter Rising of 1916, Máire and her sister Róisín were sent far from danger to the Irish-speaking Aran Islands; they spent the tumultuous years of the War of Independence and the Civil War at boarding schools.

Máire's immersion in Irish language and history from childhood had already made her a keen amateur folklorist. She graduated from UCD with a BA in Celtic Studies and joined her father's political party, Cumann na nGaedheal, where she worked for the next ten years as a secretary, journalist and sub-editor.

When, in the 1920s, Swedish academics came to Ireland to learn Irish, they marvelled at the fantastic wealth of folklore to be found in the country and they persuaded Irish academics to form a body to preserve it for future generations. Astonishingly, despite the depth and antiquity of oral heritage in Ireland, before 1930 there had never been a government-funded folklore society, but now the need to preserve Ireland's disappearing oral heritage had become urgent.

In 1935 Máire seized her chance to become a professional folklorist by joining the new Irish Folklore Commission (or Coimisiún Béaloideasa Éireann).

Over the next fourteen years, Máire recorded her findings across the country. Her research included everything from ancient relics and ruins, to customs around birth and death, to religious and supernatural lore, to herbalism and homemade medicine, to place names, surnames and the supernatural.

Máire was one of only two full-time staffers at first, but the commission grew in size and enthusiasm with the help of part-time folklorists and volunteers in the field, and thousands of storytellers across the country, some of whom could remember more than 500 tales. Over time, the Irish Folklore Commission has succeeded in amassing one of the world's richest resources of folklore. Máire published her first book *Wayside Death Cairns in Ireland* in 1946.

In 1949 Máire married John Sweeney, a Harvard University academic, and moved to Boston, USA, where she lectured in the Department of Celtic Studies at Harvard.

Máire is probably best known for her 1962 book *The Festival of Lughnasa*, which was a detailed but accessible examination of the pre-Christian, Celtic festival still celebrated in Ireland today around the end of July/beginning of August. The pagan god Lugh is thought to have started the festival to honour his foster-mother Tailtiu, an earth goddess. It represents a struggle between two supernatural powers: the dark powers of Crom Dubh to keep the first fruits and corn of the harvest for himself alone, and the generous efforts of Lugh to share food with humankind. In the seventh-century poem, we see the importance of berries and roots for sustenance as the hermit Marbhan describes to his brother, King Duaire, the bounty of nature:

Fairest princes come to my house
A ready gathering:
Pure water, perennial bushes,
Salmon, trout.

A bush of rowan, black sloes.
Dusky blackthorns,
Plenty of food, acorns, pure berries,
Bare flags.

A clutch of eggs, honey, delicious mast,
God has sent it:

Sweet apples, red whortleberries.

And blaeberries.

Ale with herbs, a dish of strawberries

Of good taste and colour,

Haws, berries of the juniper,

Sloes, nuts.

From 'King and Hermit' in *Ancient Irish Poetry*, Kuno Meyer (1913)

Lughnasa had, for millennia, involved communities coming together, often on mountainsides, to compete in games, cut the first corn, light bonfires and trade animals, in order to represent in human terms the struggle between the gods. Wild bilberries, also called blaeberries or, in Irish, *fraocháin*, were especially significant; they were picked by the young people on Fraochan Sunday, as Lughnasa is also known. As part of a courtship ritual, young men could make the plant into a temporary bracelet and present this to a young woman – but she had to take care to leave the bracelet behind her at home-time as an offering to the gods. The berries that were carried home were made into cakes for young women to eat, but it was bad luck to go back and pick more berries after 1 August. The *fraochan* also gave its name to townlands, such as Gortnavreaghaun (field of the bilberries) in Co Clare. Inevitably Lughnasa was rebranded as a Christian festival after the coming of Patrick.

The book was the culmination of twenty years' fieldwork, and earned Máire a doctorate (D.Litt.) from the National University. It can be claimed that Máire is partly responsible for the resurgence of this and other ancient

Máire MacNeill Sweeney and her brother-in-law, Michael Tierney, standing underneath a portrait of her father, Eoin MacNeill, in University College Dublin, 1964.

rituals and festivals in the late-twentieth and twenty-first centuries that contribute so much to Ireland's cultural heritage.

In 1967, Máire and John relocated to Corofin, Co Clare. She translated two books from Irish to English – *Sí-Scéalta ó Thír Chonaill* or *Fairy Legends from Donegal* (1977), and *Leabhar Sheáin Í Chonaill*, or *Sean O Conaill's Book* (1981). She wrote *Máire Rua, Lady of Leamaneh,* a biography of a fierce seventeenth-century aristocrat, which was published posthumously.

Not only did Máire make a valuable contribution to Irish culture all her working life, but when she died in 1987, she gifted her collection of modern art, including *Still Life with a Mandolin* by Picasso, to the National Gallery of Ireland, where it now forms part of the permanent collection. A fellowship in the curatorial department of the gallery has been named in her honour.

MAEVE BINCHY
1939–2012

Novelist, playwright, short-story writer and columnist

'There are no makeovers in my books. The ugly duckling does not become a beautiful swan. She becomes a confident duck ...'
Maeve Binchy, interview with *The Chicago Tribune* (1999)

Born in Dalkey, Co Dublin, just before World War II, Maeve was a rare talent – an extremely popular fiction writer, whom the literary world also recognised as a gifted chronicler of women's lives at a time of great change.

She was the eldest of four children, and the Binchy parents were affectionate, middle-class, and aspirational. After obtaining a degree in history from UCD (University College Dublin), Maeve went to work as a teacher, but she soon got itchy feet, and left Ireland to work and travel.

She claimed on her website that she had a particularly seamless entry into writing, which occurred when she wasn't even in the country. In the days before emails, the weekly letter home was the main way of communicating with family back in Ireland. Maeve's letters to her parents were so long and so entertaining that her father took them to a local paper and had them published. This was her entry into travel writing. When she returned

Popular writer Maeve Binchy.

to Ireland, Maeve became a journalist for *The Irish Times*.

Maeve published her first novel, *Light a Penny Candle* in 1982, after previously publishing collections of short stories. It was an immediate commercial success – although publishers had rejected it five times. She went on to publish another fifteen novels in her lifetime, selling millions of copies worldwide. (Her last book, *A Week in Winter*, was published after her death.) Among her most popular novels are *Circle of Friends* (1990) and *Tara Road* (1998), both of which were adapted for film. Maeve's lively stories are sympathetic portrayals of women in contemporary Ireland, as they deal with love or the lack of it, work, family, emigration and bereavement. Many of the same characters pop up time and again in the novels.

Maeve was a regular contributor to *The Irish Times* and *The Irish Independent*; she published twelve short-story collections, four works of non-fiction, and a number of novellas, plays, and radio dramas. Many of her short stories have been adapted to radio dramas and made-for-TV films.

As a young woman, Maeve had resigned herself to singledom (she was an imposing figure of a woman standing at over 6 ft tall). But instead she had a famously happy marriage to English writer and BBC producer Gordon Snell. The two even wrote, side by side, in the same room.

She herself was not interested in fame, she said, her reward being the letters she got about characters she'd written, who seemed so real to her readers. However, she did receive plaudits in her lifetime including lifetime achievement awards on both sides of the Irish Sea, a Person of the Year award (2000), and various Irish popular fiction awards. There is also a library garden dedicated to Maeve near her home in Dalkey, and a portrait by Irish artist Maeve McCarthy, which showed in the National Gallery of Ireland. And her biggest award of all? The forty million books she sold, which were translated into thirty-five languages across the world.

Maeve was crippled with painful arthritis for the last decade of her life, and suffered heart problems. When she died at home, aged seventy-two, tributes poured in, from her legions of fans, and from other prominent writers including Colm Tóibín, John Banville, Jilly Cooper and Roddy Doyle.

DID YOU KNOW?

✳ ✳ ✳

Tyrone woman **Susanna Centlivre** (1667–1723) gained an education at Cambridge University by dressing in boy's clothing and hiding in the college. She became an actress, then a playwright, then married a royal chef and became the centre of a literary circle. She was celebrated in her day, the first Irishwoman to be successful as a playwright abroad.

✳ ✳ ✳

The famous **Brontë** sisters, **Charlotte, Anne and Emily** acquired their aspirational surname from their father who had been born plain Patrick Brunty, or Prunty, in Emdale, Co Down. They lived such isolated lives in England that they spoke with a strong northern Irish accent. Charlotte married an Irish curate and honeymooned in Ireland.

✳ ✳ ✳

'**Eva of the Nation**' was the pen name of Co Galway native **Mary Eva Kelly** (1825–1910). She acquired her nickname from her popular nationalist poetry. She fell in love with her future husband just before he was transported to Australia, and she married him the day after he returned, five years later. She emigrated with him to Australia in 1860, returned to Ireland in 1885 to support Parnell's Home Rule Bill, then left again in 1888 after its defeat. Eva lived to see the publication of her poems to great acclaim in America before her death.

✳ ✳ ✳

The Honourable Emily Lawless (1845–1913) of Co Kildare was the daughter of a peer, had a family tree littered with titles, and was a staunch unionist, yet her work was much admired by nationalists. (Her 1890 novel, *With Essex in Ireland*, was written in Elizabethan English, and was so convincing that Prime Minister Gladstone believed it to be a primary source from the sixteenth century!) Her most famous poem is 'After Aughrim'.

* * *

Sinéad de Valera, née Flanagan (1879–1974), did not take part in public life, instead devoting her time to her husband, children and grandchildren. However, in her eighties, Sinéad embarked on a new career as a children's author. By the time of her death aged ninety-five, she had published ten collections of Irish fairy stories.

* * *

The acclaimed Dublin-born novelist **Elizabeth Bowen** (1899–1973) was one of the first women to write about the Irish War of Independence (1919–1921) in her novel *The Last September* (1929). It was written from the viewpoint of members of her own Anglo-Irish background.

* * *

The celebrated Galway-born novelist **Eilís Dillon** (1920–94) was also a playwright. Eilís staged *A Page of History* in 1964 at the National Theatre shortly before it moved back onto the site of the old Abbey, which had been destroyed by fire.

* * *

ARTS AND CRAFTSWOMEN

'I am without roots, but if I have any, they are in Ireland.'
Eileen Gray

EILEEN GRAY

1878–1976

Pioneering architect and furniture designer

'I am without roots, but if I have any, they are in Ireland.'
Eileen Gray

The genius of Eileen Gray went largely unrecognised until towards the end of her long life when she became, and remains, a cult figure.

Born the youngest of five at Brownswood House, near Enniscorthy, Co Wexford, Eileen's family was grand, but somewhat unconventional. Her father was the free-spirited artist James Maclaren Smith, who left the family when Eileen was a child. Her mother was Baroness Eveleen Gray, a Scottish title which, unusually, was inherited by women. Eveleen changed her children's surname from Smith to Gray when Eileen was ten, and Eileen's older sister inherited the title on their mother's death. Eileen hated being the Honourable Eileen, and never used her title.

After a ramshackle education at home by governesses in the rundown Brownswood, Eileen took her first step to freedom, aged eighteen, when she went to the Slade in London to study fine art, in the footsteps of many an aristocratic Irish girl before and after her, including Constance Gore-Booth and Grace Gifford. Eileen stayed at the family house in South

Eileen Gray in the 1920s.

Kensington, under the beady eye of her mother.

In 1900 she went travelling for the first time to study art. She had a riotous time with other well-heeled young people, taking tours around France, North Africa and Spain – and trying to avoid the many suitors who tried to claim her. She settled in Paris in 1902, where she stayed for most of the rest of her life.

By the time Eileen was thirty she had rejected the world of fine art in favour of furniture. Eileen's attention was particularly caught by the Japanese art of lacquer work. She was largely self-taught, poking about in workshops until she knew what to do, and yet she became one of the first European experts in the craft.

She was innovative, original and talented – but she was a woman, and it wasn't until 1913, aged thirty-five, that she was able to hold her first solo exhibition. At the outbreak of World War I, she dropped her burgeoning career and drove ambulances. When the Armistice came in 1918, she took up her work again.

In the inter-war years, Eileen experienced a rich period of design innovation and personal exploration. She was bisexual, having a number of affairs with both men and high-profile women through the 1920s. One of her partners, Marisa Damia, was a household name in France as one of the country's most famous singers. Eileen, however, never stayed with a partner for long.

As the 1920s went on and the Art Deco movement took off, Eileen became a leading light with her lacquered screens and cabinets. She moved on to making chrome tubular furniture and eventually designing whole interiors. She opened her Paris studio in 1922, and became a successful

Eileen Gray's house design, E1027, *in the south of France.*

businesswoman, selling her own carpets, furniture and interior design, including the now world-famous Bibendum chair, and adjustable table, which are in production to this day.

The extraordinary Eileen, then aged over forty, next taught herself architecture. In collaboration with Le Corbusier, she designed a holiday complex, and with her lover, the architect Jean Badovici, designed and built two houses in the south of France. One of the houses, known as E1027, was completed in 1929 when Eileen was fifty-one, and is regarded as one of the first Modernist classics. But Eileen had to wage war against her ex-lover for the right to be recognised as its architect, a battle which she finally won after forty years.

After World War II Eileen became reclusive and worked mainly on furniture. But following a resurgence of interest her in the 1970s, first among fashion designers and then among interior designers and architects, Eileen Gray achieved cult status.

She died in Paris, aged ninety-eight, and today the National Museum of Ireland have a permanent exhibition devoted to her. Her work is also shown in MOMA New York and in the V&A London. In 2009 her early 'dragon chair' was sold at the Christie's Yves Saint Laurent et Pierre Bergé auction in Paris for more than €20 million – the highest price ever paid for a piece of twentieth-century furniture.

EVIE HONE

1894–1955

Painter and stained-glass artist

*'Her dedication to art in all its forms was the centre of her
practical life.'*

James White, Secretary, Evie Hone Memorial Exhibition (1958)

Evie Hone was not just an internationally renowned stained-glass artist but also a talented and respected oil painter.

Eva Sydney Hone was born in Clonskeagh, south Dublin. The youngest of four daughters, she was named for her mother who died within days of giving birth to her. Her father was a director of the Bank of Ireland, but the Hones were descended from the artists Nathaniel Hone the Elder and the Younger.

At age eleven Evie contracted polio, an infectious viral disease, which blighted her childhood and that of many others before the advent of a national vaccination programme in the 1950s. Evie survived, but polio left her with a permanent disability, a partially paralysed hand and a limp she endured for the rest of her life.

As a teenager, she lived in London and split her time between attending an exclusive Harley Street clinic and studying art under Walter Sickert at

Evie Hone at work in her Dublin studio, 1950s.

the Westminster School of Art. Despite needing daily care with personal needs, such as washing and dressing, Evie continued her studies in the conventional way, by going on an art tour that took in France, Italy and Spain, and copying the great masters. At this time she became fascinated with the beauty of the illuminated manuscripts of medieval Irish monks.

Evie became lifelong friends with another fledgling Irish artist, Mainie Jellet, and through the 1920s, the two became less interested in representational art and more interested in colour and avant-garde art movements, particularly the work of Albert Gleizes. But the quirky individuality in Mainie and Evie's first Dublin exhibition of abstract art in 1924 was too much for the art establishment, and they were roundly criticised.

Evie had a strong religious faith and spent two years trying to become an Anglican nun in Cornwall, but she left them in 1927 before taking final vows. Back in the outside world, she remained a deeply spiritual person; from 1930, she found expression for this through making religious-themed stained-glass windows. In 1937 she converted to Catholicism.

In 1935 Evie joined An Túr Gloine (The Glass Tower), a stained-glass and mosaic co-operative particularly concerned with the Celtic Revival. Margaret and Harry Clarke also worked at An Túr Gloine; Harry is probably Ireland's best-known stained-glass artist, while Margaret's previously under-regarded work in portraiture is now firmly in the spotlight.

While at An Túr Gloine, Evie concentrated on the innovations she could bring to the traditional craft of stained glass. She represented her country in the Irish Pavilion in the New York World's Fair in 1939, with one of her most famous windows, *My Four Green Fields*.

Evie continued working at An Túr Gloine until 1943. From 1944 she set up a combined home and studio in part of May Guinness' house in Rath-farnham. She found she was able to combine abstraction with figurative art in her windows, and express both her Irish identity and her religious inter-ests. Commissions flooded in during the Emergency period of World War II, a nail-biting time for a stained-glass artist. Often, due to the shortage of petrol, Evie found she was transporting windows around the Dublin area by pony and cart.

Evie was recognised in her own lifetime. She received an honorary doc-torate from Trinity College in 1953 and became an honorary member of the Royal Hibernian Academy in 1955. Today there are Hone windows in ecclesiastical and academic buildings in Britain (famously in Eton College Chapel) and in the USA (Washington Cathedral), but especially all over Ireland, where Evie was keen to keep her work. *The Head of St John* (1949), *The Cock and Pot,* also known as *The Betrayal* (1947), and *Heads of Two Apos-tles* (1952) are all in the National Gallery in Dublin.

SYBIL CONNOLLY

1921–1998

World-famous Irish fashion designer

'I like to buy my mink and diamonds myself.'
Sybil Connolly, *Daily Mail* (1957)

Inspired by her love of traditional Irish hand-made fabrics, Sybil put Irish fashion on the world stage for the very first time.

She was born in Swansea, South Wales, to a Waterford father and a Welsh mother. After her father died when Sybil was a teenager, she and her mother moved to Waterford to be near his family. She was educated in a Sisters of Mercy convent school, and as soon as she left school she studied dress-making in London. It was here that she got her first taste of *haute couture*, when she was asked to assist at a fitting for the Dowager Queen Mary in Buckingham Palace.

At nineteen Sybil escaped London in the Blitz by moving to Dublin to work for the fashion house Richard Alan. Here, she worked first as a manager and then as a director, and instigated for the first time the use of Irish fabrics, such as lace, crochet, tweed and her trademark linen. In 1953 came her big moment. The career-maker and editor Carmel Snow came to visit. She loved Sybil's designs and championed them back in America. In the August of that year a dark-haired Irish colleen wearing Sybil's Irish fabrics

Sybil Connolly, 1953.

graced the front of *Life* magazine with the heading 'Irish Invade Fashion World'. Sybil had arrived.

In 1957 she moved to an 18th-century townhouse in Merrion Square, one of the smartest addresses in Dublin, and started her own couture label. Her trademark pleated linen dresses (Sybil didn't do trousers) became a must-have in the suitcases of women rich enough to travel extensively, and her sales rocketed. Through the 1960s her customers included America's richest, including First Lady Jackie Kennedy and movie legend Elizabeth Taylor.

But fashion moves on as fashion must, and no one can stay at the top for long. Through the 1970s and '80s, Sybil's designs barely moved with the times, and they fell out of favour. She accepted it gracefully. Merrion Square was still the last word in good taste with its antiques and silk wallpaper, and Sybil capitalised on her high-end reputation by creating a number of profitable sidelines – a series of highly illustrated books, as well as lifestyle items to go with her clothes, inspired by Georgian designs on ceramics, crystal and other luxury goods.

After she died of a heart attack, aged seventy-seven, the auction that took place in her beloved Merrion Square became a major society event with thousands attending. It was the last big show for Ireland's first fashion legend.

DID YOU KNOW?

* * *

The Co Kilkenny watercolourist **Mildred Butler** (1858–1941) was a member of not one but two top academies: the Royal Academy and the Ulster Academy of Arts. She painted full-size canvases, but was also famous for producing a tiny 1:12-ratio painting for a Dolls' House, on show at Windsor Castle.

* * *

Estella Solomons (1882–1968) was a gentle painter with a backbone of steel. She was a member of the Ranelagh Cumann na mBan and hid IRA men in her studio during the War of Independence (1919–21). As a member of a venerable Dublin-Jewish family, she had to wait until she was forty-seven and her parents were dead before marrying her non-Jewish husband.

* * *

According to the *Irish Independent* (2014), the dynamic paintings of Dubliner **Mary Swanzy** (1882–1978) made her 'the first Irish Cubist'.

* * *

One of Ireland's best and most original stained-glass artists, Leitrim-born **Wilhelmina Geddes** (1887–1955), battled lifelong poverty, loneliness and mental illness, including a six-month stay in a psychiatric hospital in London. It is said that she intensely disliked the work of her professional rival Evie Hone.

* * *

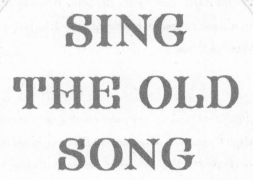

SING
THE OLD
SONG

'May the turf rest light and green above you,
Ireland's sweetest songstress.'
Irish Standard, Minneapolis (1861)

CATHERINE HAYES

1818–61

Ireland's first international opera star

'May the turf rest light and green above you,
Ireland's sweetest songstress.'
Irish Standard, Minneapolis (1861)

Catherine Hayes was Ireland's first prima donna. Born in Patrick Street, Limerick, in 1818 (though she later claimed 1825 for professional reasons), Catherine and her mother and sister were abandoned by her father Arthur Hayes, a musician.

The story of talent is inevitably to be spotted by a patron, and Catherine's exceptional soprano voice was heard during a concert in Limerick by Church of Ireland cleric Bishop Knox, who raised funds to have Catherine trained in Dublin. She made her first professional stage appearances in what is now the Gate Theatre in 1839.

Three years later Catherine had earned enough money to go abroad to study singing, first in Paris and then in Milan. She soon became a sought-after professional, creating a sensation wherever she went, including at La Scala opera house, the greatest in the world. She sang the major lyric lead roles, including the title role in Donizetti's *Lucia Di Lammermoor* and Desdemona from Verdi's *Otello*. She also had operas written for her. She was

Catherine Hayes, c.1853.

especially praised for the range of her voice, which could attain top Cs and Ds with ease, yet was also thrilling in the lower register of a contralto – a highly unusual combination.

In 1849, by then the leading soprano of her day, Catherine's presence was requested at Buckingham Palace to sing in front of Queen Victoria. It was said that Her Majesty was more taken with Catherine's quaint Irish airs than her virtuoso operatic arias.

Unlike her successor on the world stage, Margaret Burke Sheridan, Catherine chose the concert room above the opera house – and an American tour over European success. When she made plans to go on tour, London's *Musical World* magazine of January 1851 bemoaned the loss of their 'Irish Swan':

That Catherine Hayes will take Yankee-land by storm we have no doubt ...
May she not be lost on the prairies, or consumed by the effulgence of one
of Barnum's comets, but return to us light of heart and weighed
down by dollars ...

In early 1852, accompanied by her mother, she arrived in New York. Managed by none other than the great circus impresario, PT Barnum, she performed all over the country – including many gold-rush townships in California. One of her most popular encores was the Irish ballad *The Last*

Rose of Summer, which according to *The New York Herald* 'electrified the house to an extent never surpassed by the wildest applause given to Jenny Lind (the Swedish Nightingale)'.

The Last Rose of Summer

'Tis the last rose of summer,
　　Left blooming alone;
　　All her lovely companions
　　Are faded and gone;
　　No flower of her kindred,
　　　No rosebud is nigh,
　　To reflect back her blushes,
　　　Or give sigh for sigh.

I'll not leave thee, thou lone one,
　　　to pine on the stem
　　Since the lovely are sleeping,
　　　go sleep thou with them.
　　Thus kindly I scatter
　　　thy leaves o'er the bed
　　Where thy mates of the garden
　　　lie scentless and dead.

So soon may I follow
　　when friendships decay
And from love's shining circle
　　the gems drop away.

When true hearts lie withered
and fond ones are flown,
Oh who would inhabit
this bleak world alone?

Thomas Moore, set to a traditional tune *Aisling an Oigfear*

It is said that Barnum paid Catherine an astonishing $50,000, making her one of the highest paid performers of her day. In Sacramento he raffled a ticket for her first night, which went for $1200!

After America, Catherine toured Australia, India, Indonesia, and Singapore before finally settling in England. In 1857, in London, Catherine married New Yorker William Bushnell, who had co-managed her American tour. Tragically, William, who was already a sick man, died just ten months later. There were no children (but Catherine was a great-great-aunt to Irish American acting legend Helen Hayes).

Today a soprano in her forties is considered at the top of her game with solid years of training behind her and many years of performance still ahead, but for Catherine her star was already waning. She had vowed that being married would not stop her prima donna career, but being widowed did. For the next two years, Catherine performed on smaller stages.

While she was staying at the house of a friend in Sydenham, Kent, Catherine died suddenly, possibly of a stroke. She was aged just forty-three. She left £16,000 in her will, a large amount for a female performer to have accrued in her lifetime. She is buried at Kensal Green Cemetery, London. *The Times* of September 1861 recorded the loss:

We have not merely to condole with her warm-hearted compatriots, who saw no wrong in anything she did, who applauded her foreign and worshipped her national song, but with the British public ... who have lost a national favourite.

A contemporary engraving of Catherine Hayes, complete with crinoline and corset, performing the title role in Donizetti's Lucia di Lammermoor.

MARGARET BURKE SHERIDAN

1889–1958

International opera star

'Miss Sheridan is Irish, but either by luck or
instinct she sings as an Italian …'
Corriere della Sera (1919)

T he raw talent of Margaret Burke Sheridan transformed her from Maggie from Mayo to La Sheridan of La Scala.

Margaret was a descendant of the many-branched Sheridan family, who were Catholic landed gentry. Maggie was born the youngest of five children in less-exalted but comfortable circumstances, the last child of a postmaster and his wife in Castlebar, Co Mayo. The substantial three-storey post office where she was born can still be seen in Castlebar today.

Margaret's mother died of flu when her youngest child was five; at the age of eleven her father died of liver cancer. Fortunately he had made provision for her education, which continued at a convent boarding school in Eccles Street, Dublin. After the death of her father, Margaret's siblings were dispersed and her home sold. The convent became her home for the next twelve years.

Margaret Burke Sheridan on An Post's commemorative stamp, 1989.

Her voice was talent-spotted by a nun, who happened to be a music specialist. Mother Clement Burke recognised that Margaret had not only an amazingly emotional and powerful voice, but the dramatic personality to go with it. She sent her to study with one of Ireland's premier music teachers, Vincent O'Brien.

After Margaret left school, she started winning Feis Ceoil singing competitions. (The organisation still runs a Margaret Burke Sheridan competition in her memory.) The family money had run out and these were the days before music bursaries or scholarships. Therefore, Maggie's life was to consist of a series of patrons, and her first was an Irish bene-factor named Lady Palmer, who paid for her to study at London's Royal Academy of Music.

Margaret always went 'home' to Eccles Street in the holidays. One year, under the guise of singing to the nuns, it was noticed that she was actually trying to sing out of the window, hoping to attract crowds outside. The concerts were moved to the back of the convent.

She was dependent on performing in society circles in England and on the generosity of titled patrons. In the run up to World War I, aged twen-ty-five, she was still penniless. She went home to Ireland to consider her options over the summer; on returning to London, she met the famous inventor Marconi, and her life changed.

Marconi and his Irish wife, the Honourable Beatrice O'Brien, daughter of the fourteenth Baron Inchiquin, took the young Maggie under their wing. He insisted she come with them to Italy and there introduced her to society. Margaret had fallen in love with the magnificent world of opera and no longer wished to perform in smaller concert halls and drawing rooms.

She started operatic training with the respected teacher Alfredo Martino – it was a shock to her in her late twenties to be told to forget everything she knew and start learning about voice all over again. Years of technical training followed, about breathing, posture, colour of voice, mouth shape, acting, musicianship, and physical stamina.

In Rome in 1918 Margaret finally got her break. She was asked, in an emergency, by the famous director Emma Carelli to do the lead female role of Mimi in a production of Puccini's tearjerker *La Bohème*. She learned the role in four days and performed it triumphantly, making it her own. The following year she repeated the role in the Royal Opera House, Covent Garden, taking over from none other than arch-diva, Dame Nellie Melba. A prima donna had been born.

The Italians adored Maggie and always billed her as 'Margherita', but she refused to change her surname, which stayed Sheridan.

'Margherita' spent the 1920s glamorously flitting between singing engagements in the world's greatest opera houses, La Scala, Milan, and the Royal Opera House, London. She also made recordings, not only of the great soprano arias by Puccini and Verdi, but also of the Irish traditional songs of her youth. Now in her thirties, she was at the peak of her career and scaling the heights of fame, but doing it all alone, not the first or last opera star to find lasting love elusive. She fell for the MD of the Royal Opera House and they had a relationship for many years. But he was married and not about to get divorced. Margaret had to let him go.

In 1930, due to her lack of technique in the early years, Margaret experienced every opera singer's worst nightmare when her voice started to let her down on the high Cs and Ds that had thrilled so many. She lost confidence.

She gave up performing, and returned to Ireland in 1937 – it was still home, even though she hadn't been back for fifteen years, and she now spoke in a mixture of English and Italian.

She became one of Dublin's most recognisable characters, beloved of actors, singers and society. She knew everyone, the McBrides, the de Valeras, Micheál Mac Liammóir, the Cusacks. She socialised relentlessly, sponsored by those happy to keep her in the Shelbourne in the diva-esque style to which she was accustomed. She spent a lot of time on holiday in America.

It was a long and somewhat lonely retirement, but she was known for her wit and *joie de vivre*, which never failed her. She survived breast cancer but eventually succumbed to cancer of the spine in a Dublin hospital in 1958. She is buried in Glasnevin Cemetery, where part of her tombstone reads:

Margherita Sheridan

Prima Donna

La Scala and Covent Garden

MAUREEN O'HARA

1920–2015

Actress, singer and businesswoman

'My heritage has been my grounding, and it has
brought me peace.'
Maureen O'Hara

Flame-haired, flashing-eyed and feisty, in the 1940s and '50s, Maureen O'Hara was many people's ideal of the archetypal Irishwoman – especially in America, where she spent most of her long life.

Maureen was born into a middle-class family named FitzSimons in Ranelagh, South Dublin. Her father Charles Stewart Parnell FizSimons came from a prosperous family of farmers in Co Meath, and her mother Marguerite Lilburn was a singer and fashion designer. Maureen had five siblings, four of whom went into showbiz, either in front of or behind the camera; her brother helped found the Producers' Guild of America. The fifth sibling became a nun.

Maureen was 'starry' right from the beginning, with an ambitious stage mother who pushed her into roles and performances from the age of six. She won drama competitions and *féises* all over Ireland, and when she was fourteen she got her first big break when she was invited to work in the Abbey Theatre, Dublin – not as a lead, much to her disappointment, but as 'third spear-carrier on the left' in classical plays. Three years later, an invitation arrived to do a screen-test at London's Elstree Studios, and Maureen, accompanied by Mrs FitzSimons, gleefully embarked on her long exile from Ireland aged just seventeen years old.

Although she worked with and learned much from geniuses, such as Alfred Hitchcock and Charles Laughton (who was responsible for changing her name to the snappier O'Hara), Maureen was a determined young actress with a sense of her own destiny. She didn't stay long in England; London was merely a stop-off to Hollywood. By the time she was nineteen she was signed to RKO Pictures and had embarked on a movie career that was to last sixty years.

The studio system of Hollywood ensured that actors earned their money. They had to shoot at least one movie every year, do publicity all over the States, and they had to look, dress and speak a certain way. From the studio's viewpoint there was also the problem of expensive damage limitation when their stars went off the rails. Maureen was one of the more sober actresses – no drink or drug problems there – but she somehow managed to contract a teenage marriage that she kept secret, even from her mother, while en route to Hollywood. Her studio had it annulled before word got out, and she suffered no career-ending damage to her reputation. She went on to marry twice more, and gave birth to a daughter in 1944.

Maureen's most famous films include *The Hunchback of Notre Dame* (1939), *How Green Was My Valley* (1941), *Miracle on 34th Street* (1947), *Rio Grande* (1950), *The Long Gray Line* (1955), *Our Man in Havana* (1959), *The Parent Trap* (1961) and, of course, *The Quiet Man* (1952). This much-loved classic was not just Maureen's own favourite, but remains popular today, with

Maureen O'Hara remained lifelong friends with John Wayne, her co-star in
The Quiet Man *(1952).*

its beautiful Mayo backdrop, its comic quirkiness, and its famous fight scenes, all underpinned by the storyline of a strong Irish woman (Maureen) meeting her match in an even stronger Irish-American man (John Wayne). It was directed by the legendary John Ford, who Maureen claimed was either in love with her or with Mary Kate Danaher, the character he created for her in the film.

Maureen's achievements over her long life are enviable. Always a singer, she released successful albums including *Love Letters* and *Maureen O'Hara*

Sings Her Favourite Irish Songs. When her third husband died in a plane crash, she was made president of his commercial airline, the first woman in America to hold this role. As well as running her husband's airline, she also personally edited its magazine. She had a star on the Hollywood Walk of Fame, and was made Grand Marshall of the famous New York St Patrick's Day Parade at the age of seventy-eight. She co-wrote her autobiography, *'Tis Herself,* which became a bestseller. She received a large number of Lifetime Achievement awards, including an Honorary Oscar.

Maureen never lost her love of Ireland. She kept dual citizenship of Ireland and of the United States, and she had a holiday home at Glengariff, Co Cork, where she lived fulltime after retirement during her late seventies and eighties. In 2013, memory loss and increasing ill health forced her to return to live with family in Idaho, where she died two years later, aged ninety-five.

KITTY LINNANE
1922–1993

Irish traditional musician

'Wonderful, wild and exciting music ...'
RTÉ presenter Tony MacMahon (1981)

The area around Kilfenora, north Clare, has long been regarded as the home of traditional céilí music, and when Kathleen O'Dea was born in the district, she was born into a long line of musicians on her maternal Lynch side. Her mother's brother had founded a céilí band known as the Kilfenora Band, which went from house to house for weddings, wakes and everything in between.

Kitty, who had learned to play keyboards at a young age, was still at school when she started playing with her uncle's band. The hard times of the 1930s and '40s saw the band falter. It was not alone in so doing; at this time it seemed that the future of Irish traditional music, beloved of the ordinary people but disparaged in more elevated circles, was in mortal danger.

Kitty married a local man Tommy Linnane when she was aged twenty-one and went on to have six children. In 1953, a national organisation known as Comhaltas Ceoltóirí Éireann was founded to try to preserve and promote Irish traditional music, and Kitty saw her chance to revive the

Kitty Linnane at her beloved piano, taken during the band's eighty-fifth anniversary celebrations in 1992, when they played live on RTÉ radio.

band. She gathered together Lynch family members and other musicians. Led by Kitty, the new Kilfenora Céilí Band won the All-Ireland Championship at the Fleadh Ceoil in 1954, 1955 and 1956.

Kitty remained secretary and main organizer of the band for the next forty years and saw it become not only a household name in Ireland, but also in demand for tours and recordings in Ireland and Britain. As rock music hit Ireland, traditional céilí music dipped in popularity, but Kitty always managed to keep the band going. She was playing music herself right up until her death in 1993.

There was a time when a traditional music performance might result in more people on the stage than in the audience, but those days are over, and the band is going strong in its twenty-first-century incarnation, complete with websites, albums and international tours.

DID YOU KNOW?

* * *

Known as 'the Black Siren', eighteenth-century singer **Rachel Baptiste** was the first Irish woman of colour to achieve success and fame in her own lifetime. From Cork to Antrim, she played to packed houses, yet after her last performance in 1773, nothing more is known of her.

* * *

The popular Christmas hymn *Once in Royal David's City* was written by Dublin-born **Cecil Alexander** (*c.*1818–1895). She also wrote the favourite *All Things Bright and Beautiful*.

* * *

One of the most popular Irish-American performers of her day, Limerick-born **Ada Rehan** (1857–1916) was originally Ada Crehan, but on her first billboard, a typesetter dropped the C, and Ada learned to live with a new name.

* * *

The piano-playing sisters, Joan (1915–2000) and Valerie (1917–1980) Trimble from Enniskillen, became international classical performers in the 1940s and '50s as the **Nimble Trimbles**. Joan went on to become a composer and professor of musicianship at the Royal College of Music in London. On retirement from academia, she became the fourth generation of the Trimble family to edit the family newspaper, *The Impartial Reporter* in Enniskillen.

* * *

The internationally acclaimed female impersonator and singer **Danny La Rue** (1927–2009) was born **Daniel Patrick Carroll** in Co Cork, one of five children of a dressmaker. The family moved to London when Danny was nine.

* * *

UNHEARD VOICES

'The most important thing to realize is that everyone is capable of telling a story.'

Maeve Binchy

ELLEN HANLEY, THE COLLEEN BAWN

c.1803–1819

Murder victim

'He's proud of me [but] It's only when I speak like the poor people, and say or do anything wrong, that he's hurt ... I'm to be changed entirely ...'

Dion Boucicault, *The Colleen Bawn* (1860)

The sad story of the Colleen Bawn, the 'fair girl', has been dramatised in songs, books and plays. But it is a real story based on the tragically short life and brutal death of Ellen Hanley.

In early 1819 the motherless Ellen was a fifteen-year-old girl living at the house of her uncle, a farmer, near Ballycahane, Croom, Co Limerick. After her mother's death her father had remarried. One day a 'squireen' (a young man from the Anglo-Irish Ascendancy) came calling, and he was a rake by all accounts. He was John Scanlan, late of the Royal Marines, and an indebted gambler – and he'd been watching the very beautiful and very

The story of the Colleen Bawn inspired many dramatisations, including a silent American movie from 1911.

sweet-natured Ellen for some time.

Scanlan allowed himself to get caught in a downpour near Ellen's house one day and knocked on the door. He was welcomed with the warm hospitality typical of that part of the world. He was dried off, given food, and soon was able to go on his way back to his family's Big House nearby. But Scanlan had already done what he set out to do – caught the eye of Ellen. He came back and sought her out again and again in secret. They went for walks and he promised her marriage. It must have been dazzling to a girl so young to have a rich, handsome lover ready to take her to live in his mansion. Despite the other more likely offers for her hand that were coming to her uncle now that she was nearly old enough to wed, Elly's head was turned. She fell for Scanlan.

Scanlan then persuaded Elly that they would have to elope due to his family's opposition (whose objections, he promised, would disappear after the wedding). She would have to take the £60 her uncle was saving for her dowry – after all, it would be hers anyway when she married. This the girl did, against her better judgement, and in the dead of a midsummer night, the two left Ballycahane.

A Protestant clergyman named the Rev Dr Fitzgerald of Ballydonohoe Parish, Glin, Co Limerick, claims in a pamphlet of the time to have first-hand knowledge of what happened next.

As a seventeen-year-old, the newly qualified young clergyman was on his way to see his friend, John Fitzgerald, the twenty-fourth Knight of Glin, in Co Limerick. Travelling on a 'packet' (a passenger boat, a common method of travelling the Shannon), he says he met a remorseful Elly and got the whole story from her – how her husband was busy drinking and gambling away her dowry, how his mother would never accept her, and how miserable she was. The husband was unconscious for most of the journey and the Reverend claims Elly even begged fellow passengers to take her to America with them.

Some weeks later in late July 1819, the Reverend and the Knight were called away to town so that the Knight, as a magistrate, could settle a dispute about a handsome green silk cloak. This fine article had suspiciously come into the possession of one Maura Sullivan, the sister of John Scanlan's devoted servant, Stephen Sullivan. He was 'as bad a boy as any from here to Cork', according to the Reverend. Meanwhile, it came to light during this dispute, that Sullivan's employer's new wife, Elly, had disappeared.

A few days later, a body, tied up with rope, washed ashore at Kilrush near Money Point. The man who ferried the Reverend and the Knight downriver to investigate went pale when he saw the rope binding the body. He swore on a Bible that the rope was his own that he had lent to Scanlan and Sullivan days before. The body was so decomposed that it had to be identified by its corset as belonging to Ellen Hanley Scanlan.

The search went up over the county for Scanlan and Sullivan. Sullivan was said to have fled to America but Scanlan was found hiding in straw on his parents' property. He was charged with the murder of his wife Ellen, the motive being that he wanted to get rid of her so he could marry someone with more money. But despite the best lawyer his family's money could buy – some reports say that he was defended by Daniel O'Connell, the Liberator – Scanlan was convicted on the evidence of the rope and of the witnesses against him, who destroyed his alibi.

On the day of his hanging, Scanlan was given the distinction of travelling to the gallows by carriage. However, the horses wouldn't move so it is said that Scanlan jumped out and walked calmly to his own execution. Later, when he was standing with the rope around his neck, he was given an opportunity to admit his guilt, which he rejected. His general demeanor and his refusal to admit guilt both gave rise to a widespread rumour that he was innocent.

Meanwhile, it was discovered that Sullivan had not fled to America. Within twelve months he was apprehended on another matter and identified. He at first denied any part of the murder, but was tried and found guilty on evidence. He then claimed that, although he had actually carried out the murder, Scanlan had planned it.

Sullivan claimed the murder of Elly had taken place on 15 July 1819 on the pretext of going to visit a religious site on an island in the River Shannon. Sullivan had sailed out with Elly, and in the rocking boat had beaten her to death with the butt end of a gun. He had tied up Elly's body with the borrowed rope to weigh it down, having lost overboard a length of chain that he had brought for the purpose. The rope had broken or uncoiled, Elly's body had reappeared and that is how the crime had come to light.

Sullivan was hanged in September 1820. Unlike his co-conspirator, he was not given the courtesy of a burial – his body was given over to the medical profession for dissection.

And as for the remains of Colleen Bawn? She was buried in Burrane churchyard, near Killimer, Co Clare, in the grave of Peter O'Connell, a local hedge schoolmaster, who took pity on the poor young girl and her family. There is a memorial to her in the village.

The tragic story had a lively afterlife and inspired several novels, plays and songs. Most famously there was a very popular play named *The Colleen Bawn or The Brides of Garryowen*, written by Irish playwright Dion Boucicault and first performed in New York in 1860, before going on tour across Europe. (The plot features many of the facts of the case, including a young and beautiful bride, a cash-strapped squireen, a devoted but psychotic manservant – but it has the all-important happy ending.) A silent movie, based on the play, was made in 1911. There is also an opera, *The Lily of Killarney*, by Julius Benedict. The story has inspired several songs with the inevitable changed ending, the best known of which was popularised by the 1970s and '80s political folk band The Wolfe Tones. Street ballads in several versions have been in circulation since the 1860s. One version, from the point of view of a poor farmboy in love with the Colleen Bawn, comes chillingly close to the facts:

> To leave old Ireland far behind
> Is often in my mind,
> And wander for another bride
> And country for to find;
> But I have seen a low squireen
> Upon her footsteps fawn,
> Which keeps me near to guard my dear,
> My darling Colleen Bawn.

Perhaps the most fitting memorial of all is a large rock, known as the Colleen Bawn, in Muckross Lake, Co Kerry, which stands today as silent and solitary as poor Ellen must have felt in the last days of her brief life.

Colleen Bawn Rock, Killarney, Co Kerry.

ELIZABETH O'FARRELL

1883–1957

Nurse and revolutionary

'On the floor of the room lay three wounded volunteers ... a British soldier, a prisoner who was badly wounded, lay on a bed at the side of the room. Winifred Carney, Julia Grenan and I came in to attend to them. The soldier asked us would Pearse speak to him. Pearse said 'Certainly'. The soldier then asked would Pearse lift him a little in the bed. Pearse did this, the soldier putting his arms around his neck ...'

Elizabeth O'Farrell

Like many of the women who were involved in the Easter Rising, Elizabeth was a courier. This dangerous job – often given to women who were deemed to be below the radar of the government and also to keep them out of combat – involved cycling or driving, under the noses of the authorities, to give mobilization plans and strategy updates to outposts across the city, and in Elizabeth's case as far as Galway.

Elizabeth was born at 42 City Quay, Dublin, the younger daughter of a dock labourer and his wife. She received a standard Catholic education

Elizabeth O'Farrell.

and, on leaving school, trained as a midwife from 1920 to 1921 in the National Maternity Hospital. Along with her lifelong friend Julia 'Sheila' Grenan, Elizabeth joined the Gaelic League to learn more about her own culture. As was often the case in the years leading to Ireland's revolutionary period, this exposure to Irish culture led to a raising in nationalist, suffragist, and labour rights consciousness. Her membership of organisations included Inghínídhe na hÉireann (Daughters of Ireland), the Irish Women's Franchise League and the Irish Women Workers' Union.

Elizabeth and Sheila were actively supporting strikers and protecting their families during the Dublin Lockout of 1913, along with Constance Markievicz and others.

During the Rising three years later, Elizabeth was sent by Markievicz to James Connolly and attached to the Irish Citizen Army (ICA). She travelled between the GPO and Volunteer positions with orders, food and ammunition. When on the sixth and last day of the Rising, it became clear that defeat was inevitable, Patrick Pearse sent Elizabeth to offer the surrender to Brigadier General Lowe of the British Army, which said:

In order to prevent the further slaughter of Dublin citizens, and in the hope of saving the lives of our followers, now surrounded and hopelessly outnumbered, the members of the provisional government present at Head Quarters have agreed to an unconditional surrender, and the Commandants of the various districts in the city and country will order their commands to lay down arms.

Signed PH Pearse 29 April 1916

Nurse O'Farrell deliberately made herself only partially visible beside Patrick Pearse in this famous photograph of the 1916 surrender, but by the time the Daily Sketch *reproduced it on their front page, she had been entirely deleted.*

Carrying a white flag, Elizabeth went back and forth between the Irish side and the British side twice before the British accepted the surrender, with the threat of hostilities hanging over her all the time. In the only existing photograph of Lowe accepting Pearse's surrender, Elizabeth is partially obscured by Pearse and her face cannot be seen. Famously, the rest of her was then entirely deleted from the original photo when the image was released by the press.

The day after the surrender, Elizabeth was arrested and taken by the British forces around all the other outposts, including St Stephen's Green and Jacob's Biscuit Factory, to tell them to lay down arms. She was held briefly in Kilmainham before being released.

During the War of Independence and the Civil War, Elizabeth and Julia lived at 27 Lower Mount Street, Dublin, and continued to work for Cumann na mBan, leaving the organisation only in 1933. They bitterly opposed the 1921 treaty and raised funds for prisoners of the Free State.

Elizabeth's later life was spent working as a midwife in inner-city Dublin, though her last political speech, in support of IRA activities, was made in 1957 just six months before her death. An annual award named in her honour is given for academic excellence in midwifery by the National Maternity Hospital. There is also a monument to her at City Quay, Dublin, near where she was born. She is buried, along with her comrade and life-long companion, Sheila Grenan, in Glasnevin.

BRIDGET HITLER

c.1891–1969

Sister-in-law of Adolf Hitler

'Nowadays it's a bit embarrassing to be Mrs Hitler, but the people who know me don't mind, and the others don't matter.'

Bridget Dowling Hitler, *Daily Express* (1938)

Some in-laws are worse than others – much, much worse, as in the case of Bridget Dowling, who came from an ordinary Irish farming background, probably in Co Dublin, yet found herself in the clutches of one of the most dysfunctional families in history.

It started at the unlikely venue of the Dublin Horse Show. Bridget was a young woman of eighteen in 1909 when she attended the show with her father. A dapper dresser, wearing a smart hat and spats, and carrying a gold-topped cane, struck up conversation. He told Bridget his name was Alois and he was a rich hotelier on a tour of the British Isles.

The 1979 book *The Memoirs of Bridget Hitler*, purportedly written in Bridget's own words, describes how she fell in love with the apparently sophisticated Austrian after the two had tea together in Merrion Square, Dublin. What she didn't know and couldn't have foreseen was that Alois was the half-brother of the man who would become one of the worst genocidal maniacs in history, Adolf Hitler.

Their father, Alois Hiedler, or Hitler, had had several marriages. His second marriage had produced Alois and a sister Angela, his third produced Adolf and his sister Paula. Much has been written about this toxic family: how the children's mothers died young, how the father beat his children daily with a whip, how lying and self-aggrandisement were second nature, how Adolf had a controlling, unhealthy relationship with his own half-sister's daughter and is said to have driven her to suicide.

But in 1909, an Irish teenager was extremely impressed with her suave suitor. Her commonsensical father, however, smelt a rat and made enquiries about the man courting his daughter. Alois was soon revealed to be, not a hotelier, but a waiter and pot-washer at the Shelbourne Hotel.

It was the first of many deceptions. Under increasing pressure by her family to give him up, Bridget made her choice. She eloped with Alois to London in 1910, where the two were married.

The Dowling family came round to the marriage after the birth of Bridget's first and only child, William Patrick in 1911, named for her father. But another rift, with her new husband, was opening up – Alois called his son Willie while Bridget called him Pat. 'A little thing, perhaps,' she says in her book, 'but it might have served as a warning.'

The family moved to Liverpool and here Bridget's memoir goes on a flight of fancy. She claims that in 1912, the twenty-three-year-old Adolf came to stay – and stay and stay, for months in her own flat, giving Bridget a chance to see first-hand that he was lazy, mean, arrogant and dishonest. But this is likely to have been a lavish embroidering of the story, for Hitler, most biographers agree, never made it to Britain.

Alois, failing to provide a living for his wife and child in England, went back to Germany, claiming he would send for them when he was set up. The year was 1914. When war broke out, Alois did not return, leaving Bridget and Pat stranded.

For the next fifteen years they managed with the help of the Dowlings, and for most of that time Bridget believed that her husband was dead. But when Pat was thirteen it came to light that his father had remarried bigamously in Germany. Alois wrote to beg Bridget to admit their own marriage was illegal. She refused since this would make Pat illegitimate, and the case went to court. Bridget chose to defend her husband in writing, claiming to the court that he had somehow genuinely believed that he was free to marry his German wife. He escaped a prison sentence and became indebted to Bridget.

In 1929, in the dying days of the Weimar Republic, Pat joined his father Alois in Germany to work and to learn German. He returned to Germany in 1933 to witness Uncle Adolf, now Chancellor, running amok, and his Stormtroopers, Gestapo and SS all gaining strength. The memoir claims that Bridget was also lured to Germany and held against her will, but this seems unlikely. It's more probable that it was Pat who, while capitalising on the family name, had become a thorn in the Führer's side. The problem was that Adolf had pretended in his book *Mein Kampf* (1925) that he didn't have much in the way of a family, except for his sister Angela. An Irish sister-in-law, a half-brother and, worse, a British half-nephew were simply an embarrassment. Luckily for Pat, he got back to England before the situation could deteriorate.

In 1939, mother and son went to the USA. They went on lecture tours about 'Uncle Adolf' and when the Americans joined the war effort in 1941,

With a poster of Winston Churchill glowering at her back, Bridget Hitler stuffs envelopes for the British War Relief Society, a US-based humanitarian organisation active in the early 1940s.

Pat Hitler became valuable propaganda for the Allies. He joined the Navy in 1944, saw active service and was honourably discharged in 1947.

Bridget never went back to Ireland. After the war, she and Pat changed the name that, at one time looked to be Pat's passport to riches but was now a millstone around their necks. Living quietly as the Stuart-Houstons of the state of New York, Pat eventually met and married a German woman and had four sons. Bridget lived in a granny annexe in their grounds until she died aged seventy-eight. She was buried under her assumed name in the local Catholic cemetery at Coram, New York. Her son is buried beside her.

MARGARET HASSAN

1944–2004

Aid worker

'She is one of those slender people with a spine of steel.'
Felicity Arbuthnot, documentary maker

Charity worker Margaret Hassan was born Margaret Fitzsimons in Dalkey, Co Dublin. She moved to London along with the rest of her family as a young adult, where she met and married Tahseen Ali Hassan, an Iraqi engineering postgraduate. In 1972, the couple moved to Iraq where Margaret rose through the ranks of the British Council. She retained Irish, British and Iraqi nationality.

In 1991, the British Council closed operations and Margaret started working with CARE International, providing humanitarian relief to Iraqis during the first Gulf War. She headed up the charity from around 1992, and became a popular and respected figure. Known as Madam Margaret, she travelled across the country on aid missions. According to *The Independent* of 6 August 2008, her missions included delivering leukaemia medicines to children who had been contaminated by the use of depleted uranium (DU) weapons by western forces.

Despite her dislike of the country's dictator, Saddam Hussein, Margaret argued against the economic sanctions levied by the UN against Iraq. She worked on the ground with ordinary people, and responded emotionally, rather than politically, to those whose lives were made so difficult by the medical, water and food shortages of continuing embargos. She was opposed to the Anglo-American invasion of Iraq in 2003, which she felt would make civilian lives intolerable.

On 19 October 2004, Margaret was kidnapped by an unknown group. It seems that, after more than thirty years in Iraq, there were factions who wrongly suspected her of being a spy for the British government. There were demonstrations by Iraqi civilians outside CARE's offices demanding her return. But instead videos of her begging for her life were sent to the media. There were repeated telephone calls from the kidnappers to her husband; Margaret's family strongly maintain that the British Foreign Office did not do enough to support negotiations at this time.

Despite appeals for her release from every quarter, including Margaret's husband and siblings, the Irish government, NGOs, international charities, such as Islamic Relief, insurgent groups, and ordinary Iraqis, Margaret was murdered on an unknown date in November 2004. A video of her execution was sent to the media. In 2006 Mustafa Salman al-Jibouri was found to have some of Margaret's possessions, and was jailed for life, reduced to eighteen months on appeal. In 2009 a Baghdadi, Ali Lutfi Jassar al-Rawi, was sentenced to life in prison for involvement in her abduction and killing, but in 2010 it was admitted he had escaped the high-security Abu Ghraib prison during a riot there, and was on the run.

Margaret's body has never been found.

DID YOU KNOW?

* * *

Teenaged heiress **Mary Anne Knox** (1746–1761) from Co Derry was targeted for abduction for the purpose of forced marriage, but during the attempt, the abductor's gun went off and she was killed. Her killer was sentenced to hang but the rope broke and he had to be hanged again – this time successfully.

* * *

In 1798 **Betsy Gray** from Co Down became a heroine of the United Irishmen in the rebellion of that year. Betsy fought in a rebel battle near Ballinahinch, along with her brother and her fiancé. Her hand was sliced off by a sabre, and then all three were shot at the site by government forces. She is claimed by both unionists and nationalists and is remembered in the ballad 'Betsy Gray'.

* * *

A young immigrant named **Jennie Hodgers** (1843–1915) from Clogherhead, Co Louth dressed as a boy, called herself Albert Cashier and fought in the American Civil War. After the war she continued to live as Albert, and was only discovered on being admitted to hospital with a broken leg when she was old.

* * *

Mary Jane Kelly from Limerick was Jack the Ripper's fifth and final victim in 1888. She was also the youngest at about twenty-five years old. On the night of her murder in Whitechapel, Mary was heard singing Irish songs in her one-room home. She is buried in St Patrick's, Leytonstone, East London.

By strange co-incidence, the first and last women who were killed during Ireland's revolutionary period had uncannily similar names. In the opening phase of the Easter Rising in 1916, Carlow nurse **Margaretta Keogh** was shot dead as she tended the wounded. On the last day of the War of Independence in 1921, nineteen-year-old **Margaret Keogh** of Cumann na mBan was assassinated by a military hit squad as she was closing the door of her Dublin home.

GAELIC
BLUEBLOODS

'In a court or a castle, never be found
Without a woman to speak on your account.'
Ulster proverb

DEVORGILLA
1108–1193

Queen of Breifne, also known as the 'Helen of Ireland'

'I am that Helen, that very Helen,
Of Leda, born in the days of old.
Men's hearts were as inns that I might dwell in:
Houseless I wander to-night and cold.'
Nora Jane Hopper Chesson, 'Helen of Troy' (1896)

Was she a political schemer hoping to control the powerful office of High Kingship of Ireland, the overall ruler over many provincial kings? Or was she the dupe of two alpha males? Like the Greek classical figure of Helen of Troy, who left one husband and betrayed another, Devorgilla is judged harshly. In ancient annals, legend and poetry, she is seen as the cause of the single most destructive event in her country's history – the invasion of Ireland by England.

She was born the daughter of the provincial king of Meath and at thirteen was married off in a political alliance. Her husband was Tiernan O'Rourke (in Irish, *Tighearnán Ua Ruairc*), king of Breifne (roughly comprising the modern counties of Leitrim and Cavan). He may have been disliked by his new bride; after all, he was an ally of the clan that had divided and destroyed her family's territory. Devorgilla settled down to a privileged but imprisoned life. The years of Devorgilla's marriage were marked by one territorial dispute after another. For many years her husband O'Rourke had been a political player, constantly angling to increase his territory and influence. One of his most powerful erstwhile allies was Dermot MacMurrough (or *Diarmait Mac Murchada*), king of Leinster (and future father-in-law of Strongbow, the Norman knight destined to leave his mark on Ireland). In the early 1150s these two kings joined forces with the High King, Turlough O'Connor of Connacht, in order to defeat the O'Briens of Munster. They were successful in their mission, and O'Rourke felt at the pinnacle of his powers. In 1152, he went abroad on a thanksgiving pilgrimage, leaving Devorgilla at home.

It was at this point that something unexpected happened: Queen Devorgilla left her home and went to live with King Dermot MacMurrough.

Was she abducted, or did she willingly elope with her husband's former ally? Certainly the abduction of a high-status wife was not unheard of in Gaelic society – it could be viewed as a kind of hostile takeover or forced dynastic alliance – but the abducted women were always of childbearing age, whereas Devorgilla was in her forties, and MacMurrough even older.

The story goes that Devorgilla sent MacMurrough a note telling him it was safe to come and get her. He arrived with his warriors on horseback and took her away into the night – followed by her cattle and all her furniture, which she had had packed in a series of carts.

A seventeenth-century English translation of the Annals of Clonmacnoise claimed she was pimped to Dermot by her own brother:

According to this illustration in one of Gerald of Wales' illuminated manuscripts, Irishman killing each other was one consequence of Devorgilla's folly.

Dermot MacMurrough, king of Leinster, tooke the lady Dervorgill, daughter of ... Murragh O'Melaghlin, and wife of Tiernan O'Rourke, with her cattle, with him, and kept her for a long space to satisfie his insatiable, carnall and adulterous lust. She was procured and induced thereunto by her unadvised brother Melaghlin for some abuses of her husband Tiernan had committed.

But the twelfth-century archdeacon and historian to Henry II of England, Gerald of Wales, is highly convinced of Devorgilla's guilt, and the general untrustworthiness of all women:

No doubt she was abducted because she wanted to be and, since 'woman is always a fickle and inconstant creature', she herself arranged that she should become the kidnapper's prize. Almost all the world's most notable catastrophes have been caused by women ...

Expugnatio Hibernica, c.1189

In fact, the most likely explanation is that the abduction was a coup, arranged by Devorgilla and her brother, Melaghlin, who was by then the king of a much-reduced territory of Meath, thanks to Devorgilla's husband. The purpose of the abduction was to take revenge on O'Rourke, gaining back property, territory and allies, and putting the king of Breifne back in his place at the same time.

On his return, O'Rourke was furious – more about the insult to him personally and the loss of cattle and other possessions than any feeling for his wife. An older Brehon custom would have allowed for a divorce and for the wife's goods to go with her, but by the mid-twelfth century O'Rourke was able to lay claim on his wife's wealth.

The following year he attacked MacMurrough in Leinster and took back Devorgilla by force. They returned to their home, where O'Rourke publicly rejected Devorgilla. Disgraced and with no political or social future left, she ran away, alone this time. She took refuge in Mellifont Abbey, Co Louth.

O'Rourke continued to be obsessed by his desire to avenge the insult he'd suffered. In 1167, MacMurrough gave him 100 ounces of gold in compensation for taking his wife, hoping to draw a line under the incident and enlist O'Rourke's help as an ally once again. But O'Rourke continued to pursue his former friend, eventually driving him from his kingdom of

Mellifont Abbey, now in ruins, was the final refuge of Queen Devorgilla,
Antiquities of Ireland, *1793.*

Leinster (see Aoife, p269). The MacMurrough clan's loss led to them calling on outside help from, firstly, the Norman knights of Wales and, sec-
ondly, the king of England, and the rest is history.

Devorgilla lived in a religious setting for the remainder of her long life.
She outlived her husband, her lover, Aoife, Strongbow, and even Henry II
of England. She is remembered in the ancient Annals as the woman who
brought evil on her people.

AOIFE
1145–1188

Princess of Leinster

'Fair Eva wept, fair Eva pray'd,
And wrung her hands of snow;
Alas! her tears are little aid
Against the ruthless foe!'
Menella Bute Smedley, 'Earl Strongbow' (1856)

In Dublin's National Gallery there is a famous painting by nine-teenth-century Irish painter Daniel Maclise named *The Marriage of Strong-bow and Aoife* (1854). It is a highly symbolic depiction of a ruthless political moment that had far-reaching consequences for Ireland. The bride in the portrait, the beautiful Aoife, princess of Leinster, casts her eyes down in a metaphor of submission as Ireland itself would shortly be required to do. The groom, the Norman knight Richard de Clare, also known as Strong-bow, disrespectfully places one foot on a fallen Irish cross. All around are the tattooed bodies of slain Gaelic chieftains. This painting marks the moment the Anglo-Normans commenced their conquest of Ireland.

Irish kingdoms within modern-day Meath, Leinster, Connacht and Munster had been fighting over territory for as long as anyone could remember. King Dermot MacMurrough (or Diarmait Mac Murchada), trying to protect his kingdom in Leinster, took the unusual step of making

The Marriage of Strongbow and Aoife *(1854)*
by Daniel Maclise is one of Ireland's best-known history paintings.

his daughter Aoife his heir in the hopes of catching a powerful husband for
her and a much-needed ally for himself. She was already of minor royal lin-
eage through her mother's family, the O'Tooles, and this, plus the territory,
made her a double catch. It was not long before Strongbow, a landowner in
Wales, became interested.

By the Brehon Law in operation at the time, there were many different types of marriage – including abduction marriage, multiple marriage,
cousin marriage, and temporary marriage – but marrying off women for
political reasons was not originally part of the ancient system.

The ideal was that women maintained their independence and their own property through their marriages, and could divorce if they chose.

However, the Normans, though they took on much of Brehon Law, always put ambition above the rights of women, even one as high-status as Aoife.

In 1168 Aoife was contracted by her father to marry the stranger from across the sea, as a symbol of the union between two forces – King Dermot and Strongbow.

In 1170 Strongbow arrived with at least a thousand archers to aid his father-in-law. Their combined forces took Wexford and then Waterford. Aoife and Strongbow were married, and then Strongbow marched on Dublin. Some legends claim that Aoife became known as Red Eva, because of her willingness to fight battles on behalf of her husband.

When Dermot MacMurrough died in May 1171, Strongbow assumed the kingship of Wexford in right of his wife. His growing power and ambition caused England's Henry II to invade and bring him to heel the following year. Thus came about the domination of Ireland by its bigger neighbour for the next 800 years.

Aoife gave birth to a son and daughter by Strongbow. Her son died young and Strongbow himself was dead by 1176, leaving Aoife a widow, aged just thirty-one.

Aoife's daughter, Isabel, became the sole heir to her father's estates in Wales and England and also her mother's ancestral lands in Ireland. She went on to marry William Marshal, earl of Pembroke, and had five sons and five daughters. Folklore has it that due to a curse placed on the sons of Isabel by O'Molloy, the bishop of Ferns, they all died without male heirs but her daughters went on to marry into the English aristocracy, bringing

Trim Castle, Co Meath, was built to curb the territorial ambitions of Aoife's husband Strongbow.

to their husbands vast Irish lands and castles as dowries, and becoming cornerstones of the English aristocracy. It is through Aoife's female descendants, particularly her great-granddaughter, Maud, that she is an ancestor of today's British royal family.

MARGARET OF THE HOSPITALITIES

c.1380s–c.1451

Noblewoman and diplomat

'In a court or a castle, never be found
Without a woman to speak on your account.'
Ulster proverb

Margaret O'Carroll was known in Irish as Mairgréag an Einigh, or Margaret of the Hospitalities. In the medieval period in Ireland, the Brehon Law was the code by which people lived, and Brehon Law decreed that one of the greatest virtues of all was the diplomatic virtue of generosity. Margaret achieved fame for this in her own lifetime; she is mentioned specifically in the Annals of The Four Masters, which is unusual for a woman, and she is said never to have refused anything that she could give in charity. She is recorded as giving two feasts, which were attended by several thousand guests.

Margaret the daughter to Thady O'Carroll King of Ely, and Calvagh O'Connor Fahy's wife, a woman that never refused a man in the world anything that she might command, besides only her own body, it is she that twice in one year commonly invited all persons both Irish and Scottish ... to two general feasts of bestowing both meate and moneys and all manner of gifts, whereinto to receive gifts the matter of two thousand seven hundred beside gamesters and poor men ...

Annals, 1443–1468

The writer goes on to say the astonishing number at the feast was recorded in the rolls of the great families by the McEgan, the Brehon of the Offaly kingdom, and that is how he knows it has been accurately handed down. He records how Margaret stood on a balcony in a cloth of gold surrounded by her clergy and judges to watch her guests as they ate and drank their fill, and that she gave two solid gold chalices to the church, and that she took two orphans into her care as foster children. On the feast of the Assumption, she gave the second of the two feasts to all who had not come to the first one, which 'was nothing inferior to the first day'. This tradition of Irish hospitality and generosity is a crucial aspect of nobility in the Brehon code of the Medieval Irish – and echoes of it filter down to this day.

The Annals also claim that Margaret created roads and built bridges and churches, as well as doing many charitable works for her people.

In *c.*1445 in middle age, the adventurous Margaret embarked on a dangerous pilgrimage to Santiago de Compostela in Spain. There were terrible storms and she was one of only three people on the original pilgrimage to return alive. On her way back through Ireland, it is said she personally carried out negotiations for the exchange of at least three high-status Irish prisoners with several English prisoners held by her husband.

In retirement Margaret became the abbess of her own religious community, where she lived till death. 'Cursed be that sore in her breast that killed Margrett!' rages the writer of the Annals; from this we can infer that she died from breast cancer. The Annals record that her eldest son died the very next day.

A decorative Victorian edition of the medieval Irish Annals in which Margaret O'Carroll's hospitality is recorded.

NUALA O'DONNELL

c.1575–1650

Protector of the heir to Tír Conaill

'O Woman of the piercing wail,
Who mournest o'er yon mound of clay
With sigh and groan,
Would God thou wert among the Gael!
Thou would'st not then from day to day
Weep thus alone.
'Twere long before around a grave
In green Tyrconnel, one could find
This loneliness ...'

'Lament upon the Princes of Tir-Owen and Tir-Conaill'
(1840), translated from the Irish by James Clarence Mangan,
in *The Irish Penny Journal*

The birth of Nuala O'Donnell (or Nuala Ní Dhomnaill as she was known in Irish, not to be confused with the modern Irish language poet, Nuala Ní Dhomhnaill) could not have happened at a more tumultuous time. The English and Scottish were colonising Ulster and destroying the ancient systems of law and loyalties that had served for more than 2000 years. Nuala was the daughter of Aodh Dubh O'Donnell, also known as The O'Donnell, clan leader of Tír Conaill (in English this is Tyrconnell, or modern-day Donegal). She was born into war, bloodshed and exile.

Nuala's stepmother, Iníon Dubh, had taken over the clan leadership when her husband was old, to protect it for her sons Red Hugh, Cathbar and Rory O'Donnell until they came of age. Red Hugh, the heir, was imprisoned by the English in Dublin Castle in 1587 but escaped across the mountains in the winter of 1591 in a heroic feat of endurance that has gone down in legend. He lost half his foot through frostbite.

Iníon Dubh's main aim in life – and it became Nuala's too – was to defend her family's claim to the chieftaincy of Tyrconnell. To this end, she thought little of murdering those who attempted to usurp it, including her husband's nephew, Hugh Gavelach O'Neill, and her own stepson Donnell O'Donnell.

After Hugh's escape there was one family rival left – Nuala's cousin, Niall Garbh O'Donnell. Iníon Dubh decided an alliance between Nuala and Niall Garbh would ensure his loyalty to Red Hugh. The two were married in 1591 and Red Hugh was inaugurated as The O'Donnell in 1592.

Over the next nine years, the old aristocracy of Ulster gained support from within the country and from Spain, and came closer to driving out the English than it ever had before. Red Hugh joined forces with The O'Neill, earl of Tyrone, and waged battle at Kinsale, Co Cork on Christmas Eve 1601. It was a disaster for the Irish: the Ulster forces were hampered by boggy terrain and misty weather, the Spanish were late turning up, and Niall Garbh, Nuala's husband, went over to the side of the English. After this rout, the Ulster nobility fled back to Donegal. Red Hugh went to

Rathmullan, Co Donegal, from where Nuala O'Donnell accompanied the earls of Tyrconnell and Tyrone into exile, 1607.

Spain to look for more support but was poisoned by enemy spies in 1602.

Nuala obtained a divorce from the traitor Niall Garbh, as the ancient system of Brehon Law entitled her to do. Some sources say they had no children, but others say they had two sons, whom Nuala was forced to relinquish to their father, and one daughter, Gráinne, who stayed with her mother. After Red Hugh's death, Nuala's brother Rory claimed the chieftaincy of Tyrconnell, and was made the first earl by the Crown.

Nuala lived in Rory's household until 1607. In September of that year, the Ulster nobility including Rory, The O'Neill and The Maguire, hounded on all sides by the Crown forces, fled abroad from Rathmullan, Donegal, in an event that has been immortalised in legend and song as The Flight of

the Earls. Nuala was one of the ninety or so family and entourage who went with them in the fervent hope that they might regroup and fight their cause again with European support.

This Flight of the Earls sculpture, Rathmullan, was unveiled by former president of Ireland, Mary McAleese, in 2014.

Their journeying across Europe was fraught with dangers, both political and physical. They had to navigate their way through countries that had secret alliances with the English Crown, as well as through those that were sympathetic to the Irish cause. They could never rest for long. First France, then Spanish Flanders, then Italy, all the while living on a tiny pension granted to them by the Spanish King Phillip III.

Tragically, and probably due to poisoning by enemy spies, both Nuala's remaining brothers, Rory and Cathbar, died in 1608, as well as The O'Neill's son. In London in the same year, Nuala's husband, the treacherous Niall Garbh was imprisoned in the Tower by his erstwhile English allies. His vengeful ex-mother-in-law Iníon Dubh had implicated him in a treasonous plot. He died in prison eighteen years later.

The leadership of the clans was decimated; it was left to Nuala, the only surviving member of her family, to guard her fatherless nephews. One of these, Rory's son, inevitably named Hugh O'Donnell, was the heir to Tyrconnell, and Nuala was to spend the rest of her life defending his claim.

Meanwhile there was the pressing question of how to support herself and her nephews, as well as the two surviving sons of the late earl O'Neill. Nuala first made sure they were safe within the Irish College at Louvain in France. Then she negotiated with the Spanish Crown and was granted her brothers' pensions.

In 1614 in a desperate measure to restore young Hugh to his title and lands, Nuala secretly approached the English ambassador in Brussels. She begged for her nephew to be able to return to Ireland and take up his chieftaincy in return for future loyalty. Her offer was turned down. There was an intractable regime in London in the form of James I; the best the

King's ambassador could offer her was to return with young Hugh, throw themselves on the King's mercy and hope for the best. Nuala refused. She had seen what the Crown was capable of, and did not trust James.

Nuala brought up young Hugh, educated him at Louvain and obtained a place for him at the Archducal court in Brussels. He became an officer in the famous Irish Legion. This regiment, garrisoned in Brussels but within the Spanish service, comprised Gaelic Irish nobles, Gaelic Norman nobles, and their followers. It became known for the toughness and courage of its soldiers.

By this time Nuala was dependent on her adult nephew. She lived to see him grow up, marry and die honourably in battle for Spain in the Irish Legion in 1642. Her own death date is around 1650, and her burial place is said to be in the Irish College at Louvain. Her lonely and traumatic life has been remembered in poetry, where she is seen almost as the last woman standing after the Flight of the Earls, and deprived of the traditional comfort of other women at times of death. But the story of the Flight gave rise to popular expressions of defiance as the verses of this ballad of the 1840s (complete with misspellings of the period) show:

> Proudly the note of the trumpet is sounding,
> Loudly the war cries arise on the gale,
> Fleetly the steed by Loch Suilig is bounding,
> To join the thick squadrons in Saimear's green vale,
> On every mountaineer,
> Strangers to flight and fear,
> Rush to the standard of dauntless Red Hugh!
> Bonnaught and Gallowglass

Throng from each mountain pass!

On for old Erin – O'Donnell abu!

Princely O'Neil to our aid is advancing,

With many a chieftain and warrior clan,

A thousand proud steeds in his vanguard are prancing,

'Neath the borders brave from the banks of the Bann;

Many a heart shall quail

Under its coat of mail;

Deeply the merciless foemen shall rue,

When on his ear shall ring,

Borne on the breeze's wing,

Tyrconnell's dread war-cry – O'Donnell abu!

Wildly o'er Desmond the war-wolf is howling,

Fearless the eagle sweeps over the plain.

The fox in the streets of the city is prowling

All, all who would scare them are banished or slain!

... On with O'Donnell, then,

Fight the old fight again,

Sons of Tyrconnell all valiant and true!

Make the false Saxon feel

Erin's avenging steel!

Strike for your country – O'Donnell abu!

Traditional song 'O'Donnell Abu', lyrics by Michael Joseph McCann,

The Nation (1843)

DID YOU KNOW?

* * *

The goddess **Macha** was a Celtic three-in-one war goddess. She was also a Celtic princess who cursed the men of Ulster to suffer the pangs of labour, leaving Cúchulainn to defend the north alone against Maeve of Connacht.

* * *

The mother of one of the most photographed women in the twentieth-century world, Diana, Princess of Wales, was **Frances Shand Kydd**, née Burke Roche. She was the daughter of the Fourth Baron Fermoy of Cork.

* * *

Lady Katherine Ranelagh (1615–91) née Boyle, of Youghal, Co Cork, was not only an astute political plotter post-Cromwell, but also an amateur scientist who supported the career of her younger brother, the world-famous chemist Richard Boyle.

* * *

In the middle of the eighteenth century, a wealthy young Cork woman named **Elizabeth Thompson** ran away from her family to elope with a Spanish-Irish merchant. However, when her ship was attacked by pirates, she was sold to a Moroccan sultan Mohammed III as a concubine. When the sultan was assassinated, her son Yazid became sultan and she lived in his palace for the rest of her life.

* * *

A formidable Macha curses the men of Ulster.

GLOSSARY AND SOURCES

GLOSSARY

Aisling – An Irish language poetic genre developed in the seventeenth and eighteenth centuries.

Anglo-Irish Treaty – Signed in December 1921, this Treaty gave limited autonomy to twenty-six of the thirty-two counties of Ireland and kept the remaining six inside the UK. It led to the Irish Civil War, which erupted between those supporting it and those opposing it.

Annals of the Four Masters – A collection of medieval history texts in Irish.

Big House – The colloquial name for the country mansion of the landed Anglo-Irish gentry.

Brehon Law – Early Irish law code, passed down orally by specially trained Brehons, or judge-poets, until it was written down for the first time in the 600s. Governed domestic customs, such as marriage, land use and fosterage, and decided on compensation in criminal cases. It gave women more rights than they had under subsequent English rule and was still in place as late as the 1600s, until it was replaced by the English Common Law.

Camogie – Traditional Irish game played by women with a hurley (stick) and sliotar (ball).

Cat and Mouse Act – Parliamentary act of 1913 that allowed authorities to release seriously ill hunger-striking suffragettes only to re-arrest them once they had recovered.

Civil War, American (1861–65) – A four-year conflict between the northern and southern states of America, caused by a doomed attempt by the southern states to secede from the Union with their northern neighbours, and form their own Confederate States of America.

Civil War, Irish (1922–23) – Less than a year after the end of the War of Independence, tensions spilled over between two opposing nationalist groups over the Anglo-Irish Treaty and its partition of Ireland. The pro-Treatyites were represented by the Free State army and the anti-Treatyites were represented by the Irish Republican Army. The war lasted for eighteen months.

Cumann na mBan – The 'League of Women', formed in 1914 as an auxiliary corps to complement the Irish Volunteer Force (IVF) during Ireland's revolutionary period. Many members were imprisoned and some saw active service.

Dublin Lockout 1913 – An industrial dispute in which more than 300 Dublin employers locked out their workers rather than negotiate over pay and conditions. It caused widespread suffering.

Dublin Women's Suffrage Association (DWSA) – An influential non-militant suffragist group co-founded in 1876 by Anna Haslam.

Gaelic League – Organisation founded in 1913, to revive the Irish language and promote Irish culture, which also played a major part in the Gaelic Revival of the early twentieth century and became a focus for nationalism.

Irish Citizens Army (ICA) – A small army formed during the Dublin Lockout that espoused the ideal of an independent Irish socialist republic. It was re-activated during the Easter Rising under James Connolly.

Irish Party – Formally known as the Irish Parliamentary Party, formed in 1882 from the Home Rule movement and sat at Westminster where it espoused constitutional nationalism and limited self-government for Ireland. It was superseded by the more radical political parties of the twentieth century, such as Sinn Féin.

Irish Volunteers – A paramilitary nationalist group formed in 1913 in response to the activities of the Ulster Volunteer Force

(UVF). From August 1919 during the War of Independence, they became known as the Irish Republican Army (IRA).

Irish War of Independence – A widespread guerrilla war in Ireland arising from the bid by Sinn Féin to establish an Irish Republic following their General Election victory in 1918. Main combatants were the IRA on one side and the British security forces on the other. It lasted from January 1919 until July 1921, when a truce was called.

ITGWU – The Irish Transport and General Workers' Union, founded in 1909, was the strongest trade union in Ireland and played a major role in the Dublin Lockout of 1913.

Irish Women's Franchise League (IWFL) – The League, founded in 1908 and nationalist in outlook, aimed to obtain women's suffrage in Ireland by radical means as necessary.

IWSLGA – After winning the right to vote on local government matters, such as Poor Law funding, the Irish Women's Suffrage and Local Government Association aimed to obtain suffrage for women by constitutional means. It was non-militant and non-party in outlook.

IWWU – The Irish Women Workers' Union, founded in 1911, enabled women to negotiate over pay and conditions at workplaces, such as Jacob's Biscuit Factory, Dublin's largest employer of women.

Quakers – Previously known as the Society of Friends, this Christian movement, known for its devotion to pacifism and equality, originated in England in the mid-1600s and produced many social welfare activists.

Royal Institution – An organisation supporting scientific education and research into inventions, founded in London in 1799.

Royal Society – Founded in 1660, this society is the oldest national scientific institution in the world. It is devoted to promoting and educating around science.

Royal University of Ireland (RUI) – Founded in 1880 in response to Catholic demands for university-level education. In was replaced in 1908 by the National University of Ireland (NUI). It was the first university to grant degrees to women on the same basis as men.

Sinn Féin – An Irish republican political party, founded in 1905, and currently active.

Tailteann Games – A short-lived attempt by the Irish Free State to revive a tournament of Gaelic and other games, which had taken place from ancient times to the twelfth century.

Tithes – A tax, formerly levied by the Church, of one tenth of the population's annual produce or earnings.

United Irishmen – An eighteenth-century political organisation, consisting of Catholics, Protestants and Dissenters, which sought Parliamentary reform in Ireland. Inspired by events in France and America it evolved into a revolutionary republican organisation, leading to the failed rebellion of 1798 and direct rule from Westminster for the next 120 years.

University College Dublin (UCD) – Part of the National University of Ireland.

Union of European Football Associations (UEFA) – Organisation representing the national football associations of Europe (and beyond).

Young Irelanders – A nineteenth-century nationalist movement, inspired by a surge of republicanism throughout Europe and America, with the ultimate aim of demanding full legislative rights in an independent Parliament, and they advocated revolution. They were the first to present the tricolour flag of green, white and gold as a potential national symbol.

PRINTED SOURCES

Adam, Peter, *Eileen Gray: Her Life and Work*, London: Thames & Hudson, 2009.

Anon, *The History of Mother Seton's Daughters, Vol II*, Norwood Mass: Longmans, 1917.

Barton, George, *Angels of the Battlefield*, Philadelphia: Catholic Art Publishing, 1897.

Blackburne Owens, E, *Illustrious Irishwomen*, London: Tisley Brothers, 1877.

Brabin, Angela, 'The Black Widows of Liverpool' in *History Today*, Vol 52, Issue 10, 2002.

Brown, Max, *Australian Son: The Story of Ned Kelly*, Adelaide: Australiana Society Publication, 1949.

Carmichael, Amy, *God's Missionary*, Fort Washington: CLC Publications, 1932.

Carmichael, Amy, *Gold Cord: The Story of a Fellowship*, London: Society for Promoting Christian Knowledge, 1932.

Chambers, Anne, *La Sheridan, Adorable Diva*, Dublin: Wolfhound Press, 1989.

Churchill Sharpe, May, *Chicago May: Her Story by May Churchill Sharpe*, London: Samson & Low, 1928.

Clarke, Sister Sarah, *No Faith in the System*, Cork: Mercier, 1995.

Cousins, Margaret, and Cousins, James, *We Two Together*, Madras: Ganesh, 1950.

Crone, John S, *A Concise Dictionary of Irish Biography*, Dublin: Talbot Press, 1928.

Finucane, Paul, *Journeys Through Line and Colour*, Limerick: University of Limerick Press, 2010.

Fitzgerald, Reverend Richard, *The Colleen Bawn (The True History of Ellen Hanley)*, Tralee: *The Kerryman*, 1939.

Fox, Moireen, *Líadain and Curithir*, Oxford: BH Blackwell, 1917.

Fricke, Graham, *Ned's Nemesis*, North Melbourne: Arcadia, 2007.

Frost, Stella, ed., *Tribute to Evie Hone and Mainie Jellett*, Dublin: Browne and Nolan, 1957.

Garvey, Paul, *Queen of the Irish Fairways*, Dublin: The Liffey Press, 2009.

Gavan Duffy, Charles, *The Ballad Poetry of Ireland*, Dublin: James Duffy and Co, 1845.

Gore-Booth Eva, *The Egyptian Pillar*, Dublin: Maunsel & Co, 1907.

Grew, Sarah, *A Particular Confession Of [sic] Sarah Grew just now going to execution at St. Stephen's-Green*, Dublin: Printed by John Whalley in Arundal-Court, 1717.

Griffin, Gerald, *The Collegians; or the Colleen Bawn: A tale of Garryowen*. London: George Routledge & Sons, 1860.

Higgins Tom, *The History of Irish Tennis*, Sligo: self-published, 2006.

Huggins, Lady Margaret, *Agnes Mary Clerke and Ellen Mary Clerke: An Appreciation*. Printed for private circulation, 1907.

Jellett, Mainie, *The Artist's Vision: Lectures and Essays on Art* (Eileen MacCarvill ed.), Dundalk: Dundalgan Press, 1958.

Keller, Helen, *Teacher: Anne Sullivan Macy. A tribute*, London: Victor Gollancz, 1956.

Le Blond, Mrs Aubrey, *Day In, Day Out*, London: Lane-Bodley Head, 1928.

Leavitt, Judith Walzer, *Typhoid Mary: Captive to the Public's Health*, Boston: Beacon Press, 1996.

Little, Alan, *Lena Rice: The Only Irish Wimbledon Lady Champion*, Wimbledon: Wimbledon Lawn Tennis Museum, 1985.

Louis, Sr M, OSF, *Love Is The Answer: The Story of Mother Kevin*, Fallons, 1964.

Mac Lysaght, William, *'Death Sails the Shannon: the Authentic Story of the Colleen Bawn'*, Tralee: *The Kerryman*, 1953.

MacNeill, Máire, *The Festival of Lughnasa*, London; Dublin printed: Oxford University Press, 1962.

Mangan, James Clarence, 'Lament upon the Princes of Tir-Owen and Tir-Conaill', translated from the Irish, in *The Irish Penny Journal*, Vol 1, No 16, 1840.

Meyer, Kuno, ed. and translator, *Líadain and Curithir, an Irish love-story of the ninth century*, London: D Nutt, 1902.

Meyer, Kuno, ed. and translator, *Selections from Ancient Irish Poetry*, London: Constable Company Ltd, 1913.

Moran, Mary, *A Game Of Our Own, Camogie's Story 1904-2010*, Dublin: Camogie Association, 2011.

O'Connor, Éimear, *Irish Women Artists, 1800-2009, Familiar but Unknown*, Dublin: Four Courts Press, 2010.

O'Sullivan, Sean, 'The Work of the Irish Folklore Commission' in *Oral History*, Vol 2, No 2, 'The Interview in Social History: Part 2' (Autumn), pp9-17. Oral History Society, 1974.

Pilkington, Laetitia, *Memoirs of Mrs Laetitia Pilkington Written by Herself*, London: R Griffiths, St Paul's Churchyard, 1751.

Price, DS, *Tuberculosis in Childhood*, Bristol: John Wright and Sons, 1942.

Quinlan, Carmel, *Genteel Revolutionaries, Anna and Thomas Haslam and the Irish Women's Movement*, Cork: University Press, 2002.

Rowlands, Penelope, *A Dash of Daring: Carmel Snow and Her Life in Fashion, Art, and Letters*, New York: Atria, 2006.

Simms, Katharine, 'Ní Chearbhaill, Mairgréag [Margaret O'Carroll] (*d*.1451)', *Oxford Dictionary of National Biography*, Oxford: OUP, 2004.

Stopford Price, Dr D, *Tuberculosis in Childhood*, Bristol: John Wright and Sons, 1942.

Tiernan, Sonja, *Eva Gore-Booth*, Manchester: Manchester University Press, 2012.

Whitfield, Roy, *Frederick Engels in Manchester*, Salford: Working Class Movement Library, 1988.

Woggon, Helga, *Silent Radical – Winifred Carney, 1887–1943*, Dublin: SIPTU, 2000.

WEBSITES

Bewley, Dame Beulah, "'On the inside sitting alone"; pioneer Irish women doctors': http://www.historyireland.com/20th-century-contemporary-history/on-the-inside-sitting-alone-pioneer-irish-women-doctors.

Binchy, Maeve, 'Maeve Binchy interviews Eileen Gray in Paris': https://www.irishtimes.com/life-and-style/people/from-the-archives-maeve-binchy-interviews-eileen-gray-in-paris-1.2017662, from the 1976 original.

Blake, Debbie, 'Lilian Bland, Pioneering Aviatrix': http://womensmuseumofireland.ie/articles/lilian-bland, 2013

Clarke, Richard, 'Mary Daly': http://www.capitalpunishmentuk.org/daly.html.

Crowe, Aisling, 'Farewell to Anne O'Brien': https://www.independent.ie/sport/soccer/farewell-to-anne-obrien-the-best-irish-sportswoman-that-you-never-knew-35019225.html, 2016.

Crowe, Catriona, 'Ireland's Rebel Doctor, Dr Dorothy Stopford Price': https://www.irishtimes.com/culture/books/ireland-s-rebel-doctor-dorothy-stopford-price-1.1853930, 2014.

Drohan, Freya 'Sybil Connolly' : http://womensmuseumofireland.ie/articles/sybil-connolly.

Duggan, Miriam FMSP, 'Mother Kevin': https://www.catholicireland.net/mother-kevin-a-prophetic-woman.

Gartland, Jennifer, 'Rosie Hackett': http://womensmuseumofireland.ie/articles/rosie-hackett--2.

Hassett, Ella, 'Eileen Gray': http://womensmuseumofireland.ie/articles/eileen-gray.

Hawley, Charles C and Bundtzen, Thomas K, 'Ellen "Nellie" Cashman': http://alaskamininghalloffame.org/inductees/cashman.php, 2006.

Naughton, Lindie, 'Beatrice Hill Lowe': http://www.herstory.ie/news/2016/11/9/beatrice-hill-lowe-irelands-first-female-olympian, 2016.

O'Keefe, Alan, 'Truth about Darkey Kelly': http://www.herald.ie/news/truth-about-darkey-kelly-burned-as-a-witch-250-years-ago-but-who-was-really-a-serial-killer-27970534.html, 2011.

Parish of Kingscourt, 'Evie Hone': http://kingscourtparish.ie/evie-hone.

Roaringwater Journal (Finola), 'From Skibbereen to the Moon, Agnes Mary Clerke': https://roaringwaterjournal.com/2015/01/11/from-skibbereen-to-the-moon-agnes-mary-clerke.

Stanley, John, 'Nellie Cashman, Old West Philanthropist': https://www.azcentral.com/story/travel/local/history/2014/06/24/nellie-cashman-old-west-philanthropist/11319919.

General websites (authors unknown):

www.news.bbc.co.uk, 'Margaret Hassan': http://news.bbc.co.uk/1/hi/uk/3756552.stm, 2004.

www.clarelibrary.ie, 'Máire MacNeill': http://www.clarelibrary.ie/eolas/coclare/people/maire_macneill.htm.

www.fmsa.net (Franciscan Missonary Sisters for Africa), 'Mama Kevina': http://www.fmsa.net/index.php?option=com_content&task=view&id=119&Itemid=113.

www.herstory.ie, 'Kay McNulty, First Female Computer Programmer': http://www.herstory.ie/news/2016/11/9/kay-mcnulty-first-female-computer-programmer, 2016.

www.hiddendublinwalks.com, 'The Legend of Darkey Kelly': http://www.hiddendublinwalks.com/dublintours/the-legend-of-darkey-kelly.

www.historicgraves.com, 'Máire Bhuí Ní Laoghaire': http://historicgraves.com/inchigeelagh/co-ingl-0026/grave, 2013.

www.independent.ie, '98 Facts about Eileen Gray':https://www.independent.ie/life/home-garden/interiors/98-facts-about-eileen-gray-34725889.html, 2016.

www.irishtimes.com, 'Golf Trailblazer: Philomena Garvey': https://www.irishtimes.com/news/golf-trailblazer-with-unmatched-powers-of-concentration, 2009.

www.irishtimes.com, 'Sheila Tinney Obituary': https://www.irishtimes.com/life-and-style/people/pioneer-in-field-of-mathematical-physics-1.683814, 26 June 2010.

www.ria.ie, 'DIB Women on Walls: Sheila Tinney': https://www.ria.ie/public-engagement/dib-women-walls-sheila-tinney, 2016.

www.theguardian.com, 'Sister Sarah Clarke obituary': https://www.theguardian.com/news/2002/feb/07/guardianobituaries1, 7 February 2002.

www.link.springer.com, 'The Honourable Mary Ward': https://link.springer.com/chapter/10.1007/978-94-017-0351-2_2.

WOMEN
BY COUNTY

WOMEN BY COUNTY

CONNACHT

GALWAY

Sr Sarah Clarke, the Joan of Arc of prisons

Eilís Dillon, novelist

Mary Eva Kelly, aka 'Eva of the Nation', poet

Alice Perry, engineer

Sheila Tinney, Professor, mathematician

LEITRIM

Wilhelmina Geddes, artist

MAYO

Margaret Burke Sheridan, soprano

ROSCOMMON

Gretta Cousins, feminist

SLIGO

Eva Gore-Booth, labour activist and poet

LEINSTER

CARLOW

Harriet Kavanagh, Lady, antiquarian

Margaretta Keogh, 1916 victim

Sr Mary Agatha O'Brien

Mary O'Toole, judge

DUBLIN and DUBLIN CITY

Cecil Alexander, songwriter

Maeve Binchy, novelist

Elizabeth Bowen, novelist

Sophie Bryant, educator

Mella Carroll, judge

Sinéad de Valera, author

Violet Gibson, would-be assassin

Rosie Hackett, labour activist

Margaret Hassan, aid worker

Evie Hone, artist

Darkey Kelly, serial killer

Margaret Keogh, assassination victim

Lizzie Le Blond, mountain photographer

Máire MacNeill, folklorist and writer

Kay Mills, camogie player

Helena Molony, republican

Teresa Mulally, educator

Iris Murdoch, Dame, novelist

Anne O'Brien, footballer

Elizabeth O'Farrell, nurse and revolutionary

Maureen O'Hara, actress and businesswoman

Laetitia Pilkington, memoirist

Frances Power Cobbe, feminist

Carmel Snow, editor

Estella Solomons, artist

Dr Dorothy Stopford Price, TB pioneer

Mary Swanzy, artist

KILDARE

Emily Lawless, the Honourable, novelist

KILKENNY

Mildred Butler, artist

Mabel Cahill, tennis champ

LAOIS
Mary Daly, murderer

Anne Jellicoe, feminist

LONGFORD
May Churchill Sharpe, gangster

LOUTH
Philomena Garvey, golfer

Beatrice Hill-Lowe, Olympian

Jennie Hodgers, soldier

MEATH
Aoife, Princess of Leinster

Elizabeth Casey, aka E Owens Blackburne, writer

Devorgilla, Queen of Meath

Letitia Hamilton, artist

Kate Kennedy, trade unionist

OFFALY
Margaret O'Carroll, aka 'Margaret of the
    Hospitalities', diplomat

Kate Shelley, train heroine

Mary Ward, The Honourable, scientist

WESTMEATH
Evelyn Gleeson, craftswoman

WEXFORD
Mary Fitzgerald, trade unionist

Eileen Gray, designer and architect

WICKLOW
Averill Deverell, barrister

Mary Dwyer, supporter of United Irishmen

Mother Kevin Kearney, missionary

Jenny Wyse Power, feminist

MUNSTER

CLARE
Gobnait, St, saint

Ellen Hanley, the 'Colleen Bawn',
    murder victim

Kitty Linnane, traditional musician

CORK
Margaret Buckley, politician

Nellie Cashman, gold prospector

Agnes Mary Clerke, astronomer and writer

Anna Haslam, suffragist

Danny La Rue, female impersonator

Cynthia Evelyn Longfield,
    aka Madam Dragonfly

Annie Moore, first immigrant on Ellis Island

Máire Bhuí Ní Laoghaire, traditional poet

Ranelagh, Lady Katherine, politician

Frances Shand Kydd, mother of Diana,
    Princess of Wales

Elizabeth Thompson, slave

KERRY
Líadain, poet

LIMERICK
Catherine Hayes, Ireland's first operatic diva

Mary Jane Kelly, Jack the Ripper victim

Mary O'Connell, aka Sr Anthony, nurse

Ada Rehan, variety theatre actress

Johanna 'Annie' Sullivan, educator

Annie Walshe, murderer

TIPPERARY
Mary and Lizzie Burns, partners of Friedrich
    Engels

Lena Rice, tennis champ

WATERFORD
Sybil Connolly, designer

Ita, saint and poet

ULSTER

ANTRIM and BELFAST CITY
Lilian Bland, aviator

Lizzie Halliday, murderer

Ellen Kelly, gang mother

Ruby Murray, singer

ARMAGH
Macha, goddess

Jane Mitchel, Young Irelander

CAVAN
Charlotte Brooke, folklorist

Agnes O'Farrelly, academic

Dr Sr Mona Tyndall, missionary

DERRY
Mary Anne Knox, abduction victim

DONEGAL
Kay McNulty, computer co-inventor

Nuala O'Donnell 'of the Piercing Wail'

DOWN
Amy Carmichael, missionary

Winifred Carney, labour rights activist

Betsy Gray, 1798 heroine

Laura Thistlethwayte, lay preacher

FERMANAGH
The Nimble Trimbles, classical musicians

MONAGHAN
Margaret Skinnider, political activist

TYRONE
Susanna Centlivre, playwright

Dr Emily Dickson, first woman FRCSI

'Typhoid Mary' Mallon, medical curiosity

Annie Scott Dill Maunder, astronomy researcher

Margaret Elizabeth Noble, Hindu religious
    sister, educator and rights activist

FROM UNKNOWN LOCATIONS
Rachel Baptiste, singer

Dererca, St, saint

Catherine Flanagan, murderer

Mary Fleming, nurse

Margaret Higgins, murderer

Grace Marks, murder accessory

Aileen Turner, nurse

INDEX OF WOMEN

INDEX OF WOMEN

PICTURE CREDITS

The author and publisher thank the following for permission to use photographs and illustrative material: front cover image courtesy of Getty Images: p231 reproduced by kind permission of An Post; p137 The Banner of Trust; pp96, 192 Bridgeman Images/Private Collection; pp278-9 Carsten Krieger; p21 Colm O'Rourke and www.lilianbland.ie; p31 courtesy of the Royal College of Surgeons in Ireland; p51 Croke Park Museum; pp37-8 Dundalk County Museum; pp14, 19 Elizabeth Burnaby Main Le Blond Collection, Martin and Osa Johnson Safari Museum; p121 Franciscan Missionary Sisters for Africa; p36 Getty Images; pp217, 221 *Irish Times*; p152 iStock; p240 Tony Kearns, http://www.tonykearnsphotography.com/; p156 Kensington Library; p145 Jason Flahardy, Kentucky Digital Library/Henrietta Metcalf Performing Arts Photographic Collection; pp80 (KMGLM2012.0243), 87, 88, 252 (17PC-1B14-19) courtesy of Kilmainham Jail Museum; p168 Legends of America Photo Prints; pp 133, 134, 141, 167 Library of Congress; p127 © Joanne O'Brien/London Metropolitan University, Irish in Britain Collection; p179 Mary Evans Picture Library/Everett Collection: p229 © Illustrated London News Ltd/Mary Evans; p270 National Gallery; pp79, 105 National Library of Ireland; p212 National Museum of Ireland; p40 photographer Monire Childs & Kingston University Archives and Special Collections; p68 RCPI; pp206, 214 Shutterstock; p115 Sisters of Charity Cincinnati; p280 www.thesilvervoice.wordpress.com; p137 The Banner of Truth Trust, Sean Cunnington; p251 *The Catholic Bulletin*; p57 The Vintage Football Club, http://thevintagefootballclub.blogspot.fr; p161 State Library of Victoria Picture Collection; pp46, 53 TopFoto; p203 University College Dublin; pp26, 43, 62, 65, 78, 98, 112, 128, 139, 149, 142-143, 172, 176, 226, 231, 237, 245, 249, 257, 272 (and Andrew Parnell), 280 Wikimedia Commons.

If any involuntary infringement of copyright has occurred, sincere apologies are offered, and the owners of such copyright are requested to contact the publisher.

ALSO BY MARIAN BRODERICK

'Broderick's prose is simple and accessible, and her fascination
with her two favourite subjects – Irish history and women's studies –
jumps out from every page'
Sunday Business Post

In times when women were expected to marry and have children, they
travelled the world and sought out adventures; in times when women
were expected to be seen and not heard, they spoke out in loud
voices against oppression; in times when women were expected to have
no interest in politics, literature, art, or the outside world,
they used every creative means available to give expression to their
thoughts, ideas and beliefs.

*In a series of succinct and often amusing biographies, Marian Broderick
tells the life stories of these exceptional Irish women.*